HITTING THE Education Bullseye

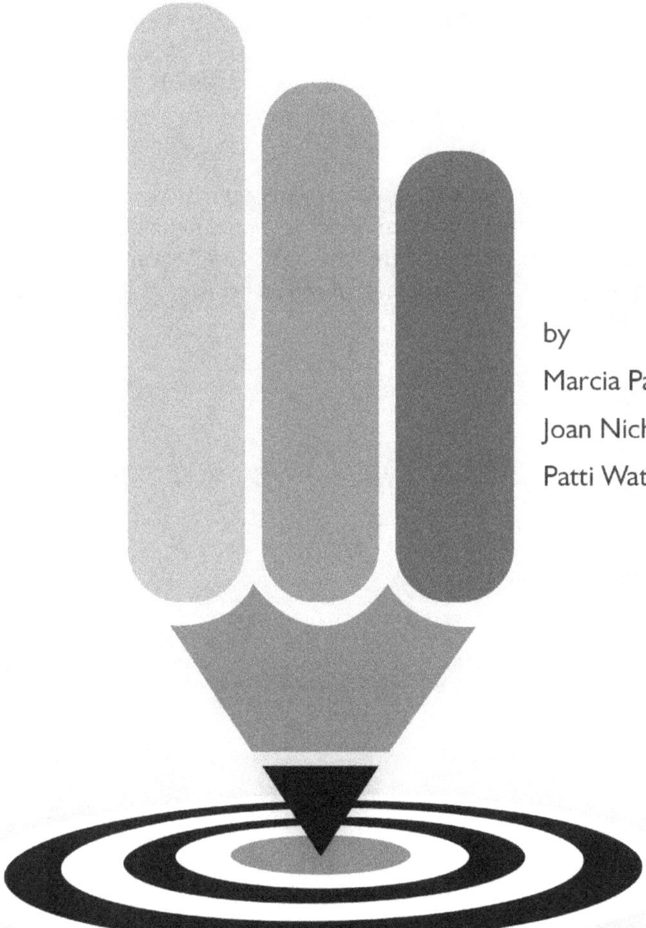

by
Marcia Page
Joan Nichols
Patti Waterbury

Adapting proven business practices to catapult great urban education from a long shot to a sure thing

© 2014 by Marcia Page. All rights reserved.

HITTING THE EDUCATION BULLSEYE
Adapting Proven Business Practices to Catapult Great Urban Education From a Long Shot to A Sure Thing

Printed in the USA.

ISBN (Print): 978-0-9864321-0-1
ISBN (Kindle): 978-0-9864321-1-8
ISBN (eBook): 978-0-9864321-2-5
Library of Congress Control Number: 2015930474
BISAC Classification: Education/Leadership

All Rights Reserved. This book is protected by the copyright laws of the United States of America. This book may not be copied or reprinted for commercial gain or profit. The use of short quotations is permitted. Permission will be granted upon request. The author guarantees all contents are original and do not infringe upon the legal rights of any other person or work.

WHAT OTHERS ARE SAYING

"*Hitting the Education Bullseye* is a wonderful primer for both the business community and the education community to develop a joint effort to drive transformative change."

—TOM LUCE
Chairman of the Board of the National Math and Science Initiative and former U.S. Asst. Secretary of Education

"Many books and endless debates have engaged the issue of what our public schools could do to better educate children (particularly poor children of color in our urban schools). None has better addressed the equally important issue of how to execute and implement transformative change. The authors of *Hitting the Education Bullseye* have actually accomplished this successfully. Without such successful implementation, plans and ideas remain dormant and offer only futile hope."

—J. MCDONALD WILLIAMS
Retired CEO, Trammell Crow Company
Chairman, Foundation for Community Empowerment

"Bringing an expertise in implementing change from the corporate boardroom to the school board and classroom, *Hitting the Education Bullseye* provides a simple, yet powerful translator to illustrate in concrete terms the applicability of tried and true change management practices to solving some of our steepest educational crises.

While business doesn't have all the answers—let's face it, no one does—successful business leaders possess a wealth of transformational experiences that educators and their leaders can glean. This book provides more than the idea, it leads teachers, business leaders, and administrators through a thoughtful series of reflections that will shed light on how to plant the seeds of positive, cooperative, silo-busting change. Albert Einstein said, "We cannot solve our problems with the same thinking we used when we created them." *Hitting the Education Bullseye* leads the reader through a first step in thinking, and acting, anew."

—DR. TIMOTHY M. BRAY

Director, The Institute for Urban Policy Research
University of Texas at Dallas

CONTENTS

7	INTRODUCTION	
	WHO WE ARE	
11	CHAPTER ONE	
	TIME FOR TRANSFORMATION	
29	CHAPTER TWO	
	OF THE STUDENT, BY THE STUDENT AND FOR THE STUDENT	
47	CHAPTER THREE	
	LEADERSHIP IS THE KEY	
61	CHAPTER FOUR	
	THE RIGHT TEAM AND THE RIGHT CLIMATE	
75	CHAPTER FIVE	
	ANALYZING HOW THINGS ARE DONE	
89	CHAPTER SIX	
	KEEPING UP WITH THE SPEED OF TECHNOLOGY	
101	CHAPTER SEVEN	
	WHERE THE RUBBER MEETS THE ROAD	
113	CONCLUSION	
	WHAT WE BELIEVE	
115	**ENDNOTES**	
121	**MEET THE AUTHORS**	
	MARCIA PAGE	
	JOAN NICHOLS	
	PATTI WATERBURY	

GOOD PROCESSES, IN BOTH BUSINESS AND EDUCATION, MAKE FOR PREDICTABLE OUTCOMES AND ARE VITAL TO TURNING A VISION INTO REALITY.

INTRODUCTION
WHO WE ARE

"Education is the most powerful weapon which you can use to change the world."
NELSON MANDELA

Transforming education is no easy task for any community. This was the goal of the Education Reform Initiative, which our team led to assist one of the nation's largest school districts. To fully appreciate the accomplishments and our involvement, it is important to understand the context in which the effort was launched and those responsible for the vision, the strategic and tactical planning and successful deployment.

The team's involvement began when the CEO and Chairman of a large corporation asked me, Marcia Page, to be a "loaned executive" working with a non-profit organization focused on building the framework and infrastructure to implement an Education Reform Initiative. The directive was simple: failure is not an option. The non-profit had convened a powerful think tank of forward-thinking business community advocates and educational leaders who planted the seeds for this ambitious goal to reform the educational process.

Given the daunting assignment to help reform public education in one of the nation's largest urban school districts, I recognized transformation in this challenging environment, especially as outsiders to the district, would require a special skill set for navigating people through change. I brought in Joan Nichols and Patti Waterbury, consultants with expertise in change management, on board to help. I focused the team on the specific goal of making a difference in the lives of children.

Though we had spent many years working together in corporate America tackling the challenges of the day and were known for tenacity and a special skill for successful implementation in the most challenging environments, this assignment would require taking the skills carefully honed in the corporate environment and applying change management principles and skills in the education industry. Recognizing the imperative of the assignment, we quickly began thinking through the differences between the public and private sector and the implications on our approach, paying particular attention to relationship building and communication.

Significant results were achieved by gaining the trust of key leaders in the district and utilizing funds from various foundations, grants, and non-profits to sustain a multi-year effort. Our small team was in place during the entire effort, providing a thread of consistency through the various phases of the project.

Over the five years we worked with the district, we came to appreciate the huge challenges educators face as well as the immense effort and commitment so vital for change in a school district. We saw firsthand the factors that differentiated schools that hit the mark from those that missed it as they adapted to change.

We have made a concerted effort to provide constructive insights regarding both. The chapters which follow illustrate how focused leadership, real collaboration and persistent follow-up are powerful influences on student and school performance.

There may arguably be as many differences among school districts as there are among businesses. Suburban schools have different problems than those which plague urban schools. Private and charter schools may have more funding and parental engagement than neighborhood public schools. Student capabilities may run the spectrum from special needs to gifted in any school. However, just as with business, at the end of the day, there are many similarities regardless of whether a school district is urban, suburban, private or charter. In spite of differences in student population, intellectual capability, demographic make-up or degree of affluence, the fundamentals of managing real transformation are the same for most school systems.

It is vitally important that business and education partner to forge a solution for what is clearly a common concern and shared passion: transforming schools to address the needs of 21st century students.

This is not a treatise on education. Educators are clearly the experts in that realm; however, principles of change are as essential in education as they are in business. Understanding them is important for any experienced educator desiring to successfully deploy pockets of excellence in education throughout school districts. This book has been written to illustrate the potential impact when business practices and change implementation expertise are combined with educator's classroom insight and "know-how" to strengthen the education system.

While definitely pleased with the success of the reform efforts within this district, we were also inspired by the dedication of educators who boldly challenged their strongest students while bending to lift the weakest. Their fierce optimism in the face of discouragement and unwavering determination to give and get the best for their students confirmed these are people who move mountains. These are the heroes; the ones who choose to help a child and make a difference. They are remarkable people.

These years have been a priceless journey for us. To impact and improve learning experiences for children is an opportunity of a lifetime; one for which we are extremely grateful.

—MARCIA PAGE,
PATTI WATERBURY AND JOAN NICHOLS

CHAPTER ONE

IT IS TIME FOR TRANSFORMATION

*"It is amazing what you can accomplish if you
do not care who gets the credit."*
HARRY S TRUMAN

I was asked to address the school reform effort for business leaders attending a civic club. Early in my presentation, I asked the mostly Caucasian, male, middle-class audience, "How many of you are products of public schools?" About 95 percent raised their hands. "So, it looks like our public schools have turned out some top-flight products," I commented, smiling at the audience. "Now, let me ask you. How many of your children go to public schools?" All but 20 percent of the hands went down.

I was not surprised by the response nor did I judge it. Yet, the reality was sobering. A large segment of our population has lost faith in our public schools and is no longer willing to entrust the system with their children.

Welcome to the 21st century. It is here. It is now. Diversity, globalization and mobile connectedness are not just buzzwords. They are reality. New, complex challenges face world leaders, business leaders and educators. The world is changing. It is not standing still.

The Census Bureau released estimates on the U.S. population's growth in 2011, finding that racial and ethnic minorities for the first time made up more than half of all children born in the country, totaling 50.4 percent compared to 25% in 1980.[1] The structure of the American family is changing with a majority of women unmarried. Over a billion people across the world are connected via Facebook, a phenomenon not even fathomed in 1980. Some 221 million Internet users in America alone have unprecedented access to information via their mobile devices.[2] There is concern about the well-being of the entire planetary climate system. The pollution in China has spread internationally as acid rain on Seoul, South Korea, and Tokyo, Japan. According to the Journal of Geophysical Research, the pollution even reaches Los Angeles in the USA.[3] Hurricanes demonstrate tumultuous changes in weather patterns. The U.S. faces economic and technological challenges unique to the changing world. The implication of these changes ripples through the United States and its schools.

TRANSFORMATION DIFFERENCES BETWEEN BUSINESS AND EDUCATION

American business leaders use proven and repeatable practices to develop products and grow profitability. In so doing, business often reinvents itself. It downsizes and hires. It insources and outsources. It automates and innovates. Business leaders do what they must to produce and to profit. When a business fails, it can be shut down, cut its losses and move on.

American business gave us the automobile and electricity at the turn of last century.[4] Later, it developed the personal computer[5] and the laser.[6] American business is known for technology and talent, productivity and efficiency, innovation and industry.

Perhaps more importantly, American business is known for its resiliency. It has learned to weather storms. During the late 1980s, U.S. businesses faced growing international competition, mainly from Japanese automakers and technology companies. As a result, in the early 1990s, American companies entered into a quality revolution that ultimately transformed their processes and their products. By 2010, successes like the Apple iPad and the invigorated auto industry proved America's ability to rebound and become global leaders in a competitive market. American public schools are now heading into the 21st century storm facing the same sort of international competition.

There are major differences between business and education. For the most part, while a business can shut down, a school system must continue to operate even when it is not successful, even when it fails to innovate or adapt.[7] Public education leaders do not have that option. A public school cannot drop low scoring math courses from its curriculum and offer only reading and science. Teachers cannot just teach kids who excel and refuse to teach low-performing students.

There are obvious and loveable differences between the output of business and the output of education; between manufacturing products and educating children. These differences, though, do not negate the immense value business practices can bring to education. Established and tested practices have made measurable differences in business and can be adapted to make measurable differences in education.

Business and education share a mutually beneficial partnership and are vital parts of the skeletal system of their communities. Businesses need an educational system that instills in their employees the skills and abilities needed to produce their products. Schools are in the business of education. They need extra funding and resources to educate their students and to produce citizens with college and career-ready skills[8] who eventually will be hired by businesses or become the future teachers of the world. When used for the benefit of public schools, business self-interest can translate into vital corporate citizenship, which improves the community and its education system.

Successes and failures in the Education Reform Initiative pointed out major differences in how businesses and school districts change and transform. However, a number of proven business practices validated they could be equally effective in education, if, and this is an important caveat, if the practices are adapted specifically to take into account each school district's unique political environment, organizational structure and diverse, and often conflicting, goals.

Throughout this book, some of the differences between education and business will be explored. In this chapter, the differences in terms of the call-to-action, responses to change and approaches to transformation are discussed.

THE BRUTAL TRUTH: TOO BIG TO FAIL! VS. TOO BIG TO FAIL?

During the 2009 bail-out of the great automakers and financial institutions, it was considered too much of a risk to the United States' economy to let them fail. They were too big to fail! Even though the education system's failing can be equally damaging and have greater long-term effects to the economy, there is not the same sense of urgency and importance given to the investment in our education. In that case, then, it is a question, is America's public education system too big to fail?

At the turn of this 21st century, the Council of the Great City Schools[9] (GCSC) reported while mathematics and reading were showing gains in urban schools, 52 out of the top 59 of the nation's large urban school districts were failing. There were 52 failing miserably at producing the type of educated children that can compete in a 21st century economy.[10] Only six urban districts had the same or higher standardized test scores than other districts in their states in all grades tested. Since then, GCSC reported in 2011, although "seven out of the nation's 10 best public high schools ranked by *Newsweek* magazine hail from urban school systems, student academic achievement is still too low[11] and dropout rates too high."

American schools did not fare any better when compared with the rest of the world. Scores from the 2009 Programme for International Student Assessment (PISA)[12] show 15-year-old students in the U.S. perform about average in reading and science, and below average in math. Out of 34 countries, the U.S. ranked 14th in reading, 17th in science and 25th in math. As another report cites, the U.S. did not lose academic ground for the 14-year period between 1995 and 2009, although more countries were improving significantly faster than the U.S. Researchers call the U.S. rate of improvement as "middle of the pack" compared with 49 countries in the following graph.[13] According to the Organisation for Economic Co-operation and Development, the Paris-based organization developing and administering the PISA exam, between 1995 and 2008 the United States slipped from ranking second in college graduation rates to 13th. "This is an absolute wake-up call for America," said U.S. Education Secretary Arne Duncan.[14]

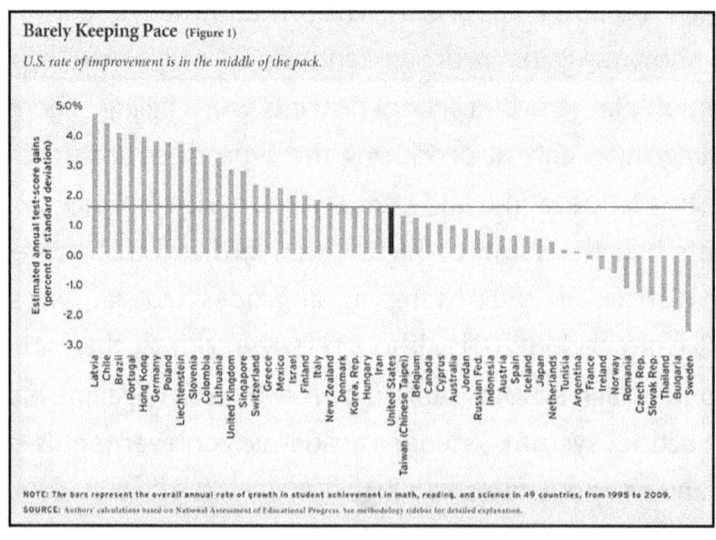

While all schools need to prepare students for the 21st century, it is the urban schools that feel the 21st century challenges more dramatically than their suburban, rural and private school counterparts. There is a difference between holding educators accountable for results and blaming them for failures that belong to society as a whole. Over 60 percent of students in the GCSC are eligible for free and reduced lunch compared to approximately 37.5 percent nationwide.[15] Cities making the greatest progress in graduation rates, such as Boston, Charlotte and Tampa, also happen to be those where community collaboration, especially with the business community, is strong.

There is a stark contrast between the environments of suburban and urban areas. Taking the exit off the freeway toward the south side schools of the pilot district, one feels transported into a different country. The trip started in the northern suburbs surrounded by manicured yards and lovely brick houses with their matching mailboxes. A bit later, stuck in rush hour traffic, magnificent downtown skyscrapers tower in every direction. Streets are crowded with well-dressed business people juggling their latest technological gadgets and favorite coffee flavor. Driving down the off ramp, suddenly signs of poverty seem to surround and suffocate. There is no immunity for the place the students call home.

Dilapidated buildings stand as physical markers of the emotional turmoil in the area. Abandoned shacks double as office space for the drug dealers who refuse to be thwarted by the boards nailed across the doors. Hints to the activity inside come in the form of used drug paraphernalia scattered among the litter scavenged by the abandoned dogs that roam the poorly maintained streets.

Grocery stores, restaurants and gas stations are few and far between. Health care facilities are limited in many areas. City transportation isn't easily accessible. The homes, apartment buildings and few businesses that do exist cover their windows with bars as a deterrent to the criminal element, but those can't stop the errant bullets fired by the numerous gangs in the area.

Like all the other buildings in the area, the school is old and in desperate need of repair. Basic utilities do not always work. It lacks playground equipment. The landscaping is comprised mostly of overgrown weeds. In small pockets, a few flowers peek out of untended gardens, simple, delicate reminders of the beauty and pride of the people who work, attend school and send their children here. For all the facility lacks, this school remains the most stable, secure place for the majority of the children who attend.

Despite this bleak picture, some schools and school programs have prevailed over challenging circumstances and overwhelming distractions. Some principals have turned their schools into safe havens for children and advocated tirelessly for their students. Dedicated teachers create the "magic" of classroom learning, day after day after day, even in the face of dwindling resources and increasing class sizes. There is goodness in public schools. The majority of Americans are products of public schools and sends their children to them. It is imperative. For the United States to move forward, Americans must promote and believe in public schools.

Nonetheless, the implication of the various assessments of education in the U.S. is jarring and not to be ignored. The failure of large urban schools is no less significant to the collective well-being than if farms were unable to produce food, power plants unable to generate electricity or automobile manufacturers unable to turn out cars. The consequences reach every level of existence: families, cities, states, country and, ultimately, the global community.

RESISTANCE AND PERSISTENCE: DO OR DIE VS. WAIT AND SEE

Resistance to change is universal regardless of business or industry. In business, implementing change can be the difference between making a profit versus shutting down operations. Switching out workers or products would be a significant endeavor for a corporation unlike a school system where every year can bring a whole new batch of students which can sometimes bring about significant change in outcomes, both positively and negatively. Although not in the best interest of the students, the impetus for change can sometimes simply mean waiting it out for the next school year. Corporations usually do not have this luxury.

There is a tendency to be immobilized by the magnitude of the problem or to abandon public education entirely for private schools. Fortunately, there are advocates actively working to find creative solutions to the challenges. The future of the children in America depends on making transformational change in education a reality.

The focus is clear. Improving the core content of education, including quality teachers and rigorous curriculum, is vital to successful educational transformation. Clearly, teaching and curriculum must excel. Teaching and curriculum are the domains of teachers, principals and administrators.

Change management experts know the business of change well. They specialize in guiding organizations through change and transformation. This is an expertise that typically does not fall into the realm of educators. This is where in collaboration with educators, change management can facilitate changes that strengthen education.

The Merriam-Webster's dictionary defines transformation as "change in composition or structure." It specifies that such change occurs in mathematics, genetics, and linguistics. However, transformation also occurs in people, cultures, social groups and organizations. In modern debate, the term transformation is now applied to education. Whether one calls it transformation, metamorphosis or "an extreme makeover," people need to understand that to educate children effectively and prepare them to compete in the 21st century, public school systems must embrace change.

There is a wholehearted and passionate belief that transformation can occur. At the same time, there is the down-and-dirty reality of the difficulty. Achieving lasting educational transformation is no relaxing stroll in the park on a spring afternoon. It is more like running a never-ending, complex obstacle course of quick turns, gut-wrenching hills and valleys and exhausting challenges. Transformation is tough and takes perseverance. It offers no quick fix, no magic wand or silver bullet. Transformation can take years. It requires continuous commitment, dedication, vision, planning and hard work.

Transformation also requires momentum, the elusive, intangible something needed to propel the effort onward. It is like the almost palpable energy surge a sports team and its fans feel when the team gets "hot" and the scores start coming fast. To sustain the momentum, though, winning just one game isn't enough. Lasting success comes from winning game after game, season after season. So it is with transformation. When the vision and the plan come together, things start moving and people start "getting it." A sense of movement and excitement is added to the commitment, dedication and hard work. This creates an energy field with enough critical mass to fend off attacks and distractions that might derail success before the change can be fully implemented.

During the Education Reform Initiative, the team was given every opportunity the district could offer along with every challenge that inevitably came with the opportunities. They worked with dedicated and passionate educators who were eager to partner for change and unselfishly gave their ideas, their time and their energy. Teachers expressed genuine gratitude for being asked their opinions. There were school leaders eager to be included in pilot programs and dedicated principals whose tireless effort reflected the importance of the initiative to their students' futures.

Of course, all was not perfect. Some educators had a bias toward the advice and expertise of perceived outsiders. Comments similar to the following were heard more than once. "You don't know what we're dealing with! You should see my 5th grade reading class! We just don't do that here."

The battle was fought against bureaucratic inertia, excuses, partisanship, politics, change avoidance and apathy. "There's no need to change things here," one teacher commented. "This, too, shall pass, and so will you."

Experiences in this school district are not unique. The desire for change is universal, as is resistance to it. These are the normal paradoxes found in transformation initiatives. The ever-present see-saw of varying perspectives results in a balancing act that is inherent in transformation and must be faced by those leading change. Leading change, even "good change" is not for the faint of heart. By harnessing the desire for change and overcoming resistance, the vision and plan for change can be created, implemented and sustained.

TRANSFORMATION MODEL:
BUSINESS VS. EDUCATION

Situations change; people transition. For change to last, the transition must be sustainable. Without a systematic approach and understanding where one is now and where one wants to be, it is difficult to produce effective change.

The Education Transformation Model provides a systematic and proven approach to effective change. It is rooted in quality improvement practices used for years by Fortune 100 companies to achieve operational excellence. The model has been adapted to meet the specific needs of school districts moving toward educational transformation. It requires an honest self-assessment of the current state and an open mind about the future state. Just as architects carefully draw blueprints when designing a new building, the model helps create a roadmap or vision for educational transformation that focuses on the 21st century student. The following graphic illustrates the model.

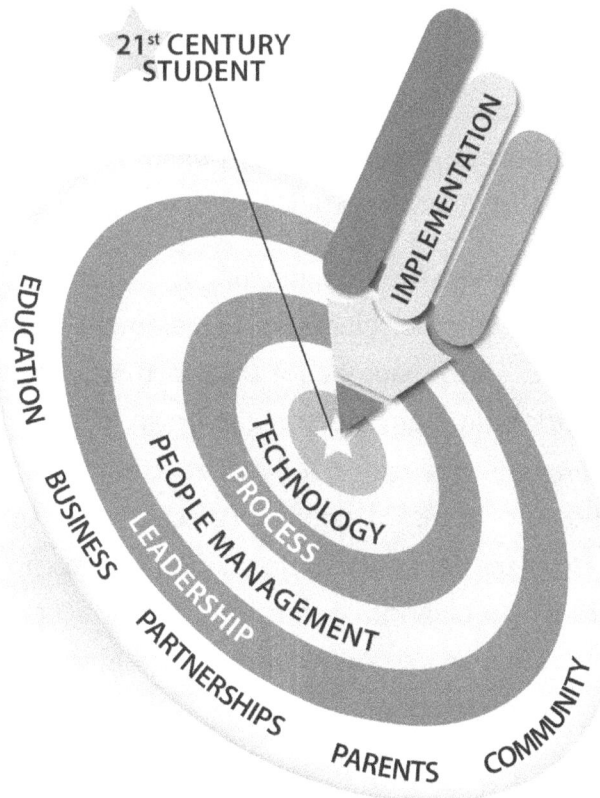

The 21st Century Student is the center, the heart, the bullseye and sole focus of the Education Transformation Model. The outer rings of Leadership, People, Process and Technology, enable student learning and ensure transformation is directly and intently focused on student success. Regardless of the product, business or organization, these four, interrelated elements must align to achieve operational excellence and transformation. A deficiency in just one of these elements can jeopardize success. The arrow represents movement or the inertia that is required for implementation to begin. Although a catalyst for change can come from outside forces, ultimately it is the superintendent who must ensure the organization is ready, aimed at the bullseye to fire the arrow for successful transformation. Education is a community, business and parental concern. A school district cannot do it alone. Partnerships across these constituencies providing resources, support and sponsorship to the school district are the foundation for successful transformation.

Each element of the model must function effectively and work cohesively with the other elements. No element can be ignored or skipped. Once the roadmap for transformation is fully drawn, the hard work of implementation can begin. Detailed plans for implementing the changes need to be created. These plans are the "how" of transformation. Project phases, budgets and timelines are all part of how transformation will be implemented. Changes must be planned, persistent, organized and carefully thought-out. Change can only happen with ongoing evaluation and consistent leadership.

The following chapters describe each element of the model in more detail. The chapters will show how each element can be impacted by the various constituencies of the school district, how they can work differently in business and education, and how these differences can influence transformation.

At the beginning of the initiative, consultants considered the Malcolm Baldrige criteria for performance excellence. One consultant had used this successfully as a basis for transforming a Fortune 100 company. The Baldrige Criteria provides a comprehensive way to achieve and sustain high performance across the entire organization. It addresses all key areas of a running a successful organization and is compatible with other performance improvement initiatives and innovative ideas.

The Baldrige Criteria are a valuable framework for measuring performance and planning in an uncertain environment. After evaluating the model, its basic concepts were used to build a strategic plan for a small church that was embarking on a journey to triple the size of their facility, staff and congregation. The model as a framework worked perfectly. After reviewing the findings, it seemed this model, with a few changes, could be adapted to fit the unique challenges and culture in education. This began the Education Reform Initiative journey.

KEY TAKEAWAYS

▶ Researchers describe U.S. academic performance of high school students as "middle of the pack" and greater challenges face the largest urban districts. The prevailing thought among education advocates is schools need transformation in order for children to meet the challenges of the 21st century and beyond.

▶ Education reform goes beyond just educators and requires collaboration across a coalition of policy-makers; education, community and business leaders; and parents and guardians.

▶ Application of change management practices in business must be modified to work in a school district.

▶ Student learning is at the center and remains the constant focus of the outer rings of the model for transformation to be successful. The chapters in this book are associated with each component of the model, but in reality are very interdependent.

REFLECTIVE QUESTIONS

▶ What are the largest challenges your school district is facing? How does your school district's academic performance compare among the best in the state, country and world?

▶ Given the 21st century challenges (economic, technology and impact of political changes in our global society), what current initiatives are you implementing in your district?

▶ How well are the initiatives across your district functioning? Where have you seen rapid improvement or status-quo challenges in your district or other high performing school districts?

▶ Are you getting the desired outcome from initiatives across your district? What obstacles do you face when expanding proven practices beyond the "pockets of excellence?" What capacity is needed to make it a reality?

RESISTANCE TO CHANGE IS UNIVERSAL REGARDLESS OF BUSINESS OR INDUSTRY.

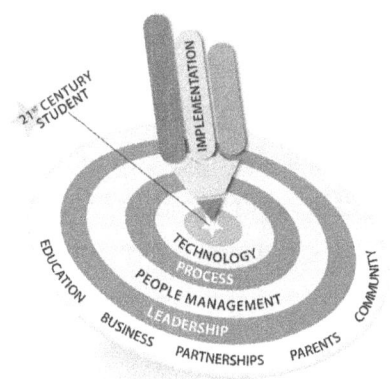

CHAPTER TWO

OF THE STUDENT, BY THE STUDENT AND FOR THE STUDENT!

"Student: 'You're a miracle worker. How did you do that?' Teacher: 'All I did was give you what I knew you needed before you knew you needed it. So thank you for the compliment but education is the miracle. I'm just the worker. I'm a teacher and that's what we do.'"

—TAYLOR MALI

The challenge articulated by a 10-year-old student to thousands of educators was simple, "Do you believe in me?" This young man had delivered a speech that rivaled most polished speakers. The video went viral immediately. He even appeared on the Oprah Winfrey Show. He came from one of the highest poverty neighborhoods and a district with a less than stellar academic record. His message was a call to action to educators. "Do you believe in all 220,000 of us ... that we can ALL be college and career ready?"

Reactions from teachers were extremely positive. For months afterwards, teachers and administrators from the pilot district recalled how moved and impressed they were by this young man's speech. They felt it should be heard by everyone involved in the education of children no matter what position they held. The challenges were thought provoking and worthy of repeating time and time again.

The speech was a memorable illustration of the potential that rests within each student to defy the odds when student learning is the focus and measure of success for a district. This young orator symbolized the potential of 21st century students to make a difference and shared wisdom beyond his years. He articulated that transformation happens one person at a time and everyone in the system needed to expect and enable student learning for things to change.

While it takes more than a speech to create a culture where everyone believes and has the discipline to be the best, believing is an important first step.

At the heart of the transformation model is the student. The ultimate test of educational transformation is a sustainable improvement in student learning. The student is the active recipient of the educational process, just as a customer receives products and services from a business. The outer rings of the model—Leadership, People Management, Process and Technology—exist solely to enable student learning and to satisfy the obligation to graduate each student as a responsible citizen, poised for success in a technology-driven, information-rich, global society.

Put in business terms, student learning is the output from the core competency of school systems, just like building a reliable vehicle is the output of Volvo's core competencies. Entertainment is the output of the Walt Disney Corporation business model while its core competencies come down to three: animation, storytelling creation and theme park operation efficiency. Successful companies are passionate and focused on being the best at their core competencies.[1]

American schools need to be passionate and focus on being the best at teaching and learning. From furniture to fitness, from lipstick to laptops, companies bombard patrons with reasons why they are the best in the world at what they do. It's an hourly, daily, winner-take-all competition for survival. It's a race to be better, newer, faster, more agile, more relevant to consumers, and ultimately, more profitable.

Historically, international competition has been intense for American businesses; but increasingly, students are encountering stiff international competition for jobs in America and abroad. In an ever-expanding global arena, the competitive stakes in education are growing. Graduates of American schools must be positioned for success as responsible citizens who can compete globally and be well compensated for meaningful jobs. Ready or not, American public schools are in a race to generate the best-educated, most capable students in the world. If American students cannot compete at the global level, how can Americans believe that U.S. schools are successful?[2]

STUDENT LEARNING AS A "CORE COMPETENCY" IN TRANSFORMATION

Everything districts, schools, and classrooms do should contribute to student learning, whether directly or indirectly. The focus, then, of educational transformation is to dramatically improve how a school system delivers teaching and learning. It all boils down to core competency. Core competencies are the foundational activities that need to be performed consistently, and performed well, in order for teachers to teach and students to learn. These competencies are performed in any classroom and supported at the school and district levels. There are many frameworks educators have to measure this, but the framework designed and developed by the National Center for Educational Accountability[3] encompasses the core competencies in education and provides a database of proven practices from high-performing schools across the country. The framework, as well as some sample questions, is at the center of the student learning bullseye for the Education Transformation Model:

▶ **Curriculum and academic goals**

Are lesson plans derived from the set curriculum and aimed at achieving the mastery required at each grade level? Is what is supposed to be taught in each classroom being taught? Is it being graded the same?

▶ **Capacity development and collaboration**

This ultimately comes down to the teacher. Do teachers have adequate training? How are they assigned to classes?

How do they collaborate and support each other across subjects and grade levels?

▶ **Instruction delivery**

How is the lesson delivered? Does the teacher use hands-on, small groups, technology based or traditional lecture methods?

▶ **Monitoring and assessments**

How is data used to drive lessons and determine if students are grasping the subject matter?

▶ **Intervention**

If a student is not getting it, what tutoring or additional review is needed? What positive reinforcement for achievement is present?

These activities are the substance of student learning. Transformation must address and dramatically improve how these are performed in a school district in order to measurably improve student learning. District and school leaders must be the best at what they do and ardently believe that every student can learn.

"CORE COMPETENCY" DIFFERENCES BETWEEN BUSINESS AND EDUCATION

Companies differentiate themselves by the products and services they deliver. Business tries to achieve sustainable differentiation from its competition, win customers and make a profit. How well companies perform in those core competencies is reflected in their ability to sustain success in their respective marketplace. In education, it's all about teaching and learning. How well a school teaches determines how well its students learn. While business and education have different core competencies, both need to be passionate about what they do to perform and manage these competencies successfully. There are some key differences in the ways business and education measure results, assess performance against best practices and balance consistency with innovation to be the best at their core.

INFORM: FIRST-HAND VS. SECOND-HAND FEEDBACK

Successful companies measure their success not only with business results, but the health of employees, customers, and financials. Business is accustomed to measurements. Leaders measure and study everything that impacts their ability to be successful. Product quality, worker productivity, environmental footprints are a few. However, perhaps no measurements are more critical to business than market growth and profit numbers. Business measurements are fairly straightforward. Growth and profitability are either up or down.

Measuring student performance is generally not that straightforward. Although the introduction of standardized state tests has led education to measure results, it is not without controversy. Presenting complex school data in terms parents, students and the community can understand is a challenge.

Single snapshots of data about graduation rates, college readiness, special education effectiveness or English language learners are complex and often contradictory plus they seldom provide meaningful trends over time. For example, passing a standardized test does not necessarily equate to college and career readiness as determined by a college entrance exam.

Researchers did a comparison of the Texas standardized test scores against the Texas Higher Education Assessment (THEA) that measures skills freshman-level students should have for successful undergraduate work. Almost half of the 11th graders in English and only five percent in Math would be able to meet the minimum college-readiness standards with a "passing" grade illustrated in the figure below.[4]

	11th Grade TAKS Score	Predicted ACT Score	Predicted SAT Score	Approximate Probability of THEA score>230	Approximate Probability of THEA score>270
English Language Arts	2100 (Passing)	17.7	461	57%	
	2300	22.5	543	90%	
Math	2100 (Passing)	19.5	472	67%	5%
	2300	24.3	570	100%	77%

College and Skilled Career Readiness Benchmarks For All Students

"Passing" standardized tests is not adequate for college-readiness, but researchers also show that it is not adequate for workforce-readiness. As represented in the figure below from

ACT researchers, there is no difference in work versus college readiness when it comes to mastering basic subjects.[5] Most jobs profiles did not require a bachelor's degree, but did require some vocational or on-the-job-training. This is also, therefore, a measure of workforce training readiness.

Difference Between "College-Ready" and "Workforce-Ready" is Negligible

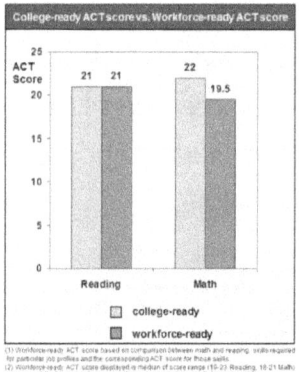

Standardized test data can measure select grade levels and subjects and the data can roll-up to measure a school's overall academic ranking. A school is considered high performing when 90 percent of the students pass the standardized state test. Yet as we have illustrated, this does not ensure students are "college and career ready." These mixed messages on student achievement metrics are not only confusing to people outside of education, but many educators and school leaders are unaware of the correlations between scores on state exams and true success.

During the pilot program, school leaders looked at standardized test data for their classrooms as compared to schools with similar demographics and the best in state regardless of demographics. The data was formatted in easy-to-read graphs. Training to interpret the data was provided since many of the teachers were unaccustomed to this type of analysis. For many of the school leaders, it was a disheartening experience and their resolve was tested. The victim mentality and the cries that "we are different," had to be dispelled before the data was accepted and true change could begin. The real feeling of competition had to be created in teachers to mirror the reality their students will face in the competitive world of the 21st century. School leaders and teachers had to believe they could change and that they had responsibility to ensure all students could be successful.

These snap shots over time do offer a way to compare performance against other schools in the state using common test results. As discussed earlier in this chapter, test results must be weighed against a higher "college and career-ready" standard or the desired outcome of schools is not achieved. Although there is more work to effectively measure success in terms of desired outcomes, test scores are a way to measure performance across schools and, hence, the effectiveness of education's core competencies.

How do we stay focused on outcomes that measure value-added improvement every year of each student? Success in education comes down to discovering what it will take for every student to consistently grow and achieve at higher levels every year so they will ultimately be prepared for the 21st century.

INSPIRE: QUICK STUDY VS. EXTENDED RESEARCH

Companies decide what they are good at based on the profitability and market growth of certain products and services. They can either divest or bolster less profitable business units so they can become the best and make the most profit. Companies, especially those in high tech industries, invest significant capital in research and development (R&D) to pilot innovative ideas and products to become the best in the world or the first to market.

Schools, on the other hand, must excel at teaching all students, poor and rich, gifted and average, English as second language learners and special education students. And they must teach every subject at every grade level. Every student must be measured by the standardized test for that grade level and that subject. Public school educators do not have the luxury to "opt out." They cannot purge a subject or drop a group of students to get better test scores. A school cannot change, delete or ignore a core subject area it falls short on in order to improve overall performance.

The ultimate goal for a school district is to improve student achievement for every student and, additionally, to close the achievement gap among low-income and minority students. For urban school districts, doing this successfully means competing for the coveted Broad Prize.[6] School districts, which want to be successful have only one option: to improve and become better at performing the core competencies required for every student to learn.

In an ideal world, a school system would only have students eager to learn, supportive parents and superstar teachers in every classroom. Unfortunately, the reality is schools may not have superstars in every classroom and students may not all come from supportive homes. Yet there are schools, which consistently outperform others with similar demographics. What causes these differences? Simply put, it comes down to a school or school district collectively understanding its core competencies and how to perform them well. It means understanding the gaps in execution and knowing how to fix them together. Where there are gaps in core competencies, successful school systems learn what is not working and invest in the capacity to make them better. A super, or even good, teacher cannot do it alone. Successful schools systems have support at the school and district levels to support the core competencies. If students are multiple grade levels behind, successful schools respond with a school-wide tutoring program to catch them up before new material is taught. If special education students are struggling, successful best practices, such as instituting a buddy program, are considered. People passionate about student learning have the courage to take the hard looks and make the improvements.

Successful school leaders tasked with improving a struggling or an already high-performing school analyze and dissect what is working and not working with their core competencies. They form leadership councils consisting of influential, forward-thinking teachers from a cross-section of subjects and grade levels. The council leads in-depth conversations to investigate and understand the core practices at their school and how they compare with other successful schools that maintain a laser-like focus on classroom learning. These schools have groups of teachers routinely looking at data, modeling lessons with each other and monitoring the execution in the classroom. They make adjustments as needed and remain undaunted in their pursuit of student learning.

IMPROVE: U-TURN VS. NO TURN

Great companies operate within established and consistent processes. Yet, also, they are agile and quick to change directions when the market or customers dictate. This is the basis for survival. Successful businesses are disciplined yet, flexible; structured yet, responsive. These characteristics can describe other professions, as well. Airplane pilots need to be meticulously diligent in adhering to flight and safety procedures yet, be competent and flexible so they can handle unexpected emergencies and devise creative, on-the-spot solutions. The same is true for surgeons, fire fighters or race-car drivers. Standard operating procedures must be deeply ingrained to produce consistent results, but competent professionals must also be flexible and able to adjust when non-standard situations occur.

The same concept applies to educators. Most urban schools deal with mobile, large and diverse groups of students. Multiple languages, unique cultures and a wide range of individual student needs are part of the variety of challenges educators face daily.

Balancing a common framework with flexibility for competent teachers to adapt yet, still meet aggressive performance goals is key. For example, following a core curriculum is important given the high mobility of students; however, the curriculum has to be flexible enough based on the student dynamics. Out-dated, "one-size-fits-all, cookie-cutter" approaches are ineffective for today's multi-ethnic environment. When school districts build infrastructures to support and re-enforce core competencies, teachers become adept at following standard procedures and they develop disciplined skills. These procedures and skills enable teachers to maintain a high level of student learning while being flexible and responsive to emerging and changing student requirements. Teachers are able to innovate, improve, and devise tailored solutions, while still performing the disciplines of their core competencies.

An innovative district leader asked the consultants to help implement a math initiative aimed at engaging students through the use of technology. Data for math scores were not trending in a positive direction. The campus leadership had collectively determined that teachers were struggling to reach students through traditional delivery methods. Results from other school districts, which had implemented the program, showed

improved math scores across all demographics. The technology allowed teachers to submit questions, homework and quizzes via the student's handheld to get a real-time read on student understanding of concepts in order to tailor the lesson for that day. Gaming, internet and technology played well into the hands of eager, tech-savvy math students, but proved to be a bit daunting for some of the teachers coming from a less-technical generation. The excitement from the students and a significant investment of training, in-class coaching and collaboration with each other enabled teachers to overcome their initial fears and ultimately reach every student, not just the outspoken ones, but the quiet and hard-to-reach students.

The next challenge was ensuring consistent delivery of the new program from class to class and campus to campus. The presence or absence of a consistently delivered curriculum can best be observed by walking from campus to campus or classroom to classroom. One doesn't have to be an educator or a curriculum expert to spot good teaching and recognize diligence to a standard curriculum. On a walk-through with a principal, two high school geometry classes were observed. In the first, the day's objective was on the board and the classroom activities clearly mapped to the objective. The teacher was sending geometry problems to the students' graphing calculators. The students worked the problems individually, talked about the answers in their small groups and then, electronically submitted their answers to the teacher and the class for further discussion. The students and the teacher were engaged; one could sense the learning going on.

The next classroom was the same. In fact, it felt like the first and second teacher were simultaneously reading from the *same script, so exact was their content and so similar were their activities. These teachers were on task and on target. Students in both classes were learning what was expected of them.*

THE STUDENT IN EDUCATION AND TRANSFORMATION

▶ District and school leaders must first believe all students can succeed then be passionate about being the best at what they do—preparing every student to compete in the 21st century with the best in the world.

▶ Standardized test results are a gauge for comparing performance with classrooms across the district and state, but must not be confused with ultimate outcome and focus to ensure every school graduates college and career-ready 21st century students.

▶ School leaders focused on a collective and deep understanding of core practices that lead to consistent results are able to create conditions that make effective teaching and learning improvements possible.

▶ Driving consistency in every classroom across the district requires discipline in addition to disseminating proven practices adapted to the unique challenges of each school and regularly monitoring the implementation to make the adjustments needed to get it right.

REFLECTIVE QUESTIONS

▶ What messages about school goals, benchmarks and accountability have been conveyed to staff? How has their role in these been articulated? How do you assess individual students and monitor progress to assure each student achieves individual goals over time?

▶ What frameworks does your district utilize to understand and improve performance against your core competencies? How do campus leaders collaborate inside and outside their campus to ensure alignment and improvement around a core set of practices?

▶ How well do transformation efforts (district and campus improvement plans) ensure that students graduate as socially responsible young adults prepared for the 21st century challenges? How does your district identify proven practices and disseminate them quickly across campuses and classrooms?

▶ How does your district monitor consistency across campuses, classrooms and balance innovation?

▶ What data is used to measure success for your schools and students across your district? How are these metrics shared with parents, educators, students and the community at large for transparency and understanding?

GRADUATES OF AMERICAN SCHOOLS MUST BE POSITIONED FOR SUCCESS AS RESPONSIBLE CITIZENS WHO CAN COMPETE GLOBALLY AND BE WELL COMPENSATED FOR MEANINGFUL JOBS.

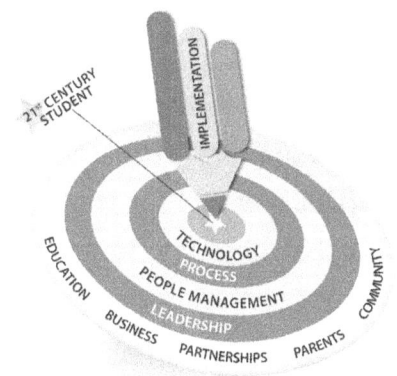

CHAPTER THREE

LEADERSHIP IS THE KEY

"If your actions inspire others to dream more, learn more, do more and become more, you are a leader."
– JOHN QUINCY ADAMS

Transformation requires an energy field to push the momentum of change forward. Creating it would be a simple task if there were Star Wars leaders like Obi-Wan Kenobi, Princess Leia and Luke Skywalker at the helm. They could create an energy field with one dramatic sweep of a light saber, invoking the power and wisdom of the "Force.' They could travel to friendly planets if they needed additional support or simply enlist the help of clever droids, like R2-D2 and C-3PO. It would be easy.

Jedi warriors, though, are not available. Traveling the galaxy with the power of the "Force" isn't an option, either. Days and nights are spent on planet earth, living lives and raising children. Options are limited to the earthly realm and each day brings joys, as well as the realities of the human condition: imperfection and self-interest. It is understandable that the dynamic, persuasive and authentic leadership needed for transformation is a highly valued and rarely found commodity. Transformational leadership might actually prove more amazing than the intergalactic abilities of superheroes. Although there aren't real Jedi warriors, there is an epic battle for the future of children. To be victorious, transformational leadership is integral.

LEADERSHIP IN TRANSFORMATION

A well-informed school district superintendent, like the business CEO,[1] is in the best position to set strategy and provide transformational leadership. In reality, CEOs and superintendents do not function in isolation or allow themselves to become a single point of success or failure. CEO and superintendent leadership must include a team of credible and trustworthy leaders who are committed to the transformation goals and use their influence and actions to inspire the organization forward. While the impetus for transformation can be external for both—competition, customers, local community or news media—true, passionate ownership of transformation can only take hold and be driven by leadership from within. Without a superintendent's leadership, educational transformation cannot occur. It cannot be delegated.

> **TRUE, PASSIONATE OWNERSHIP OF TRANSFORMATION CAN ONLY TAKE HOLD AND BE DRIVEN BY LEADERSHIP FROM WITHIN.**

LEADERSHIP DIFFERENCES BETWEEN BUSINESS AND EDUCATION

What does transformational leadership look like? Many leadership books agree that a successful leader excels in the following activities: inspiring a shared vision and strategy, setting challenging goals, enabling decision-making and accountability, communicating and shaping a culture and climate of the organization.[2]

These leadership practices work in the business world. There is no reason to think they wouldn't work in education, as well. However, what these accepted practices do not account for is the uniquely public nature of a school district. They are called *public* schools because they are owned *by the public* and the superintendent is accountable *to the public*. The simplicity of that concept belies the immense impact it has on the leadership practices of a superintendent. Basically, the concept alters the essence of the leadership required for transformation in a public school system.

A superintendent has to deal with things a CEO does not. In addition to the accepted leadership practices, the superintendent must also be adept at practices that address the "open book" of public education. To provide leadership for transformation in education, a superintendent must provide clear direction and build support inside and outside the school system to successfully implement and sustain transformation.

This is no small task, and yes, Obi-Wan Kenobi could be very useful here. Without him, the superintendent must rise to the occasion and provide the authentic leadership needed to push the school district to change and transform.

Why do these differences matter? If the superintendent or business and community leaders fail to recognize the uniqueness of leadership in education and fail to account for it in their thinking and planning, expectations will misalign and critical partnerships may not fully develop.

LEADERSHIP TRANSPARENCY: THE OFFICE VS. THE FISHBOWL

In a business or corporation, whether privately or publicly held, the decisions of a CEO are not typically open to public scrutiny. CEOs can allocate research and development dollars or approve investment. As long as the business operates legally and generates a profit, daily operational decisions are considered confidential and private. They can make decisions behind closed doors regarding daily operations of the business. CEOs can lead private lives as long as their "public" personas reflect the values and image of their companies.

In a public school system, the decisions of the school system are not only open to the community, the "business" is funded by the taxpayers and supplemented by grants or donations given with specific expected outcomes. The community feels a personal kinship, though at times unrealistic and uninformed, that demands accountability and transparency from the school district. A public school is the *public's* school, heavily influenced by their board of trustees, students, parents, the community at large, the business community, the news media and the city's elected officials. The operations and inner workings of the school system are constantly open to public scrutiny and so is the superintendent. Nothing is hidden. Nothing is protected. Everything is reported from the district's expenditures on toilet paper to the superintendent's salary, from the story of two parents' battle with the school district over the length of their son's hair to the decision to mainstream special education students into general education classes. For the superintendent, there is no privacy. Life is a fishbowl. There are no curtains, no shadows and no place to hide.

A superintendent's constituency is not the monolithic, customarily compliant group of stockholders and, to a certain extent, employees found in business. In a corporation, a CEO can assemble 300 stockholders at a meeting, deliver good or bad news and generally everyone accepts the explanation. In education, *if a district could get* 300 parents at a meeting to deliver good news, chances are only a small number will leave happy. Why? The parents might represent 30 different schools with 30 different priorities and question the relative "goodness" of the news for their students.

When a CEO speaks, information is distributed throughout the organization in a structured way according to the CEO's will. A CEO controls the message and determines the "who, what and when" of communication. A CEO rarely faces public questions except in extreme cases when egregious breaches of trust and confidence stir public outrage and thrust corporate operations into the public eye.

In contrast, anything a superintendent says can be public and can be heard by audiences intended and *not* intended to hear it. Superintendents cannot maintain the same degree of control as CEOs. A superintendent's message not only flows through the district, it also zigzags to constituents across the entire community. It flows up the political chain to the mayor, the governor or even higher. It travels as far as the statement's impact carries it. Superintendents are expected to routinely, publically address their constituents with issues and communicate unpopular decisions, such as justifying a school closing to the neighborhood, describing curriculum changes to parents, defending layoffs to the unions, explaining lower test scores to the business community, and explaining financial discrepancies to the press.

STRATEGY: SELECTION VS. EQUITY

Strategy in business involves assessing markets, competition, customers and internal capacity to determine how to differentiate the business from competitors.[3] CEOs have the responsibility to make and keep business profitable. They can pick and choose their opportunities and their product lines. They can widen or narrow their view, re-focus and grow business in areas that generate the most revenue and best support their core business. They can choose to outsource or select suppliers that can best support their strategy. Successful CEOs select only the best opportunities to maintain the most profitable, competitive edge.

In contrast, a superintendent does not have the luxury to choose the students in a school district. The community supplies these students, who are priceless commodities, needed by schools to practice their art and science of education. A public school's mission is to educate all children and to practice equity. The district not only provides education to children in the expansive middle of the bell curve,[4] it also caters to both tails of the curve—children with special needs and children who are gifted and talented performers. The school district must educate children from all racial groups, ethnic groups, and socio-economic classes in a variety of community, neighborhood, alternative, charter, and magnet schools.

GOVERNANCE: THE BOARD AND STOCKHOLDERS VS. STAKEHOLDERS

Whether it is a corporate board of directors or a board of trustees for a school district, each plays a role in selecting executive leadership and watching over the "value" of the corporation or district. In most corporations, the board of directors are in sync with company strategy and values. Board members interact with the corporate executives and reports to a captive group of stockholders.

On the other hand, a School Board of Trustees is generally voted into office and represents the community at large. The board may or may not be sympathetic to the superintendent and, if highly politicized, can significantly constrain the superintendent. The superintendent must also deal with and, hopefully, build relationships with powerful individuals or stakeholder groups. These are highly visible and vocal constituents—elected city leaders, business leaders, community leaders, parents, and students—who exert constant pressure and wield influence that in some cases is stronger and more compelling than that of a formal board.

In business, succession plans are often put in place to identify and groom future corporate leaders. The decision about who will be the next CEO is often determined internally, then approved by the board with a rubber-stamp vote by the stockholders. It is not so for education. In a school district, the superintendent is often selected and approved by the board of trustees on the recommendation of a search firm, at times without serious input from local community leaders. Often times, superintendents are brought in from "outside" without knowledge of the district's internal workings and critical relationships.[5] "Outside" leaders also tend to bring their own staff with them, further complicating matters. All of these factors contribute to a higher leadership turnover in education than in business. According to sources, CEO average tenure is 8.4 years[6] versus 3.6 years average[7] tenure

> **THERE IS A MUCH HIGHER LEADERSHIP TURNOVER IN EDUCATION THAN EXPERIENCED IN BUSINESS. THIS PRESENTS SIGNIFICANT CHALLENGES TO TRANSFORMATION.**

of superintendents from large urban school districts. This lack of continuity can stymie transformation efforts and make sustainable change out of reach.

This was certainly true during the multi-year Education Reform Initiative. The district involved had four superintendents in seven years and associated turnover of the executive leadership staff. When the initiative started, there was a supportive interim superintendent. Fortunately, there was a strong community leader with vast community resources, together with a tenured, well-respected district administrator who helped consultants navigate the terrain and continue with support for transformation efforts. If there had not been that continuity of leadership and support, multi-year reforms simply would not have been implemented.

The reality is that the average tenure of superintendents in large urban American school districts today is short at best. However, large city school districts that have shown the strongest student gains in the last decade have almost all had, and continue to have, long-serving superintendents. Superintendents who focus on the right goals, manage change effectively, and are around long enough to drive results, tend to have higher-performing students and are able to make transformations work.[8]

PARTNERSHIPS: CORPORATION VS. COALITION

Corporations and school districts both depend on contractual partnerships to help them produce their products and deliver their services. A corporation tightly controls its supply chain and develops contractual agreements covering most every aspect of it: suppliers, manufacturers, logistics providers and even customers. A corporation can choose to outsource specific operational functions, allowing its leaders and employees to focus on activities that are critical to the mission of the corporation and its core competencies. Generally speaking, corporations are able to maintain power and control over the most critical resources and partnerships they need to be competitive.

Like corporations, school districts depend on contractual agreements with vendors, suppliers and teachers, to name a few, in order to facilitate the operations of the education process. Beyond this, the similarities begin to fade. School districts require cultivation of additional partnerships because schools work with a most valuable commodity—children. Because of the children, schools are often dependent on non-profit, faith-based and community-based organizations, business foundations, and government entities for additional help and services. These partnerships exist outside of school boundaries and jurisdictions. Ironically, while they cannot be tightly controlled by the school district, these relationships ultimately contribute to the success of a school district and public school students.

Effectively building and nurturing this coalition of partnerships is a test of the superintendent's vision and leadership skills. A school district cannot do it alone. Supportive community and business coalitions provide resources and services needed to fill the gap, especially for low-income students, caused by constant budgetary constraints and restrictive regulations. Partnerships with non-profit organizations can fill the void left by families incapable of providing the mentoring their children need. Federal programs provide breakfast for hungry students. "Education is Freedom" can provide resources to assist students with identifying finances and support to successfully navigate through college and career.

Building collaborative relationships with providers in the community can be mutually beneficial in solving problems. Collaborations with quality community pre-school for toddlers can expand limited space and provide important linkages to feeder elementary schools. Trusted relationships with local universities ensure primary and secondary education programs are relevant and produce high-quality, effective teachers. Working with programs like "Teach for America" can supplement inner-city schools struggling to attract and keep quality teachers through creative contracts and financial support for college. Businesses can adopt a school or participate in cooperative efforts such as offering internships or supporting science, technology, engineering, and mathematics (STEM) programs.

Ultimately it comes down to the superintendent creating an environment where these partnerships are valued and building the coalition with parents, partner agencies, and community and business leaders around the district's transformation goals.

CHAT ROOM

As we spent time with principals across scores of campuses, we observed a general lack of support for the school leaders. We witnessed confrontational parents, read negative news articles and reviewed district mandates for doing more with less. Professional development to help these leaders typically occurred in the summer and in-school application seemed lost once the students and daily pressures returned. We came to appreciate that the school leader was in a critical and lonely position.

To try to improve these conditions, we developed an executive coaching program. Each principal was paired with a business leader based on interviews matching individual needs of the principals and the strengths and expertise of the executive. Business leaders came to the schools to provide coaching on the "business of running a school" or running a school as a "mini-business."

The principals found great value in the relationships and the support and information they provided. In addition, the executive coaches received an unintended benefit. They gained an appreciation for the principal's job and a new insight into education, which could not be gleaned from negative stories in the local news. The experience was invaluable and a "win-win" for the school leaders and the business leaders who participated.

LEADERSHIP IN EDUCATION AND TRANSFORMATION

▶ Credible and trustworthy leadership is the key to any transformation and due to the public nature of school systems becomes even more critical with both internal and external constituents.

▶ Ideally, superintendents need to simultaneously remain close to the lives and needs of the children, while garnering support for a bold vision and listening to students, teachers and principals so that transformation is possible.

▶ Boards comprised of elected officials play a critical role in selecting superintendents and focusing on creating great schools, but create challenges not typically faced by business leaders.

▶ The superintendent must have the ability to form strong coalitions with policy makers, community and business leaders who can provide resources, partnerships and energy to drive transformation efforts.

REFLECTIVE QUESTIONS

▶ What are the priorities of your district? Are they shared and supported by district and campus leaders?

▶ What key strategies have you, or high-performing school districts, successfully implemented that have achieved rapid and sustained results?

▶ Are district leaders creating a setting that embraces transparency, innovative learning or other improvement initiatives?

▶ How does your district, or other high-performing school districts, address allocation of resources to ensure all schools have what they need to meet performance goals?

▶ What types of joint partnerships exist between the district and the community at large? What are the characteristics of effective collaborations in your district or within other world-class education systems?

▶ What practices for maintaining executive leadership continuity have you seen successfully implemented in your district or other high performing districts? If leadership turnover is an issue, what practices have you or high-performing districts used to improve leadership continuity and stability?

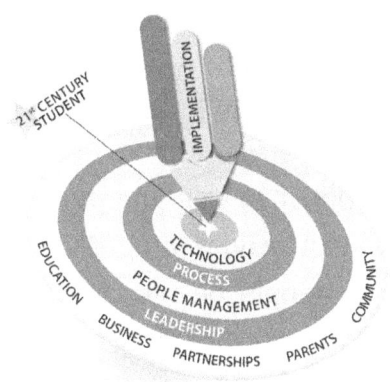

CHAPTER FOUR

THE RIGHT TEAM AND THE RIGHT CLIMATE

"True democracy cannot be worked by twenty men sitting at the center. It has to be worked from below, by the people from every village."
—MOHANDAS GHANDI (MAHATMA)

Sustainable transformation depends on authentic leadership, bolstered by a solid vision and strategy combined with strong, persuasive people practices. Great leaders and the right team make all the difference in any environment, be it a football coach and the starting line-up, a CEO and business leaders, a superintendent and executive staff, or school principals and their teachers. A superintendent can paint a compelling picture of the future, but without engaging the right people, the vision will not become reality. More to the point, the vision will lose power and so will the superintendent. Just as the quality of employees greatly impacts the value creation of a corporation, the value delivered by an education system is completely dependent on the combined capabilities of the district and school leadership.

PEOPLE MANAGEMENT IN TRANSFORMATION

As the chief people manager, the superintendent or CEO must ensure people practices are fully leveraged to attract and keep the "right people on the bus."[1] In a school system, the "right people" include not only district leaders and top administrators, but also, and perhaps most importantly, high quality and committed school leaders and teachers. Everyone knows a great teacher makes a difference. Almost everyone can remember a teacher who had a significant impact on his or her life. Passionate, self-directed educators can create pockets of excellence and significantly influence a student; however, they rarely drive change beyond their immediate sphere of control. A more deliberate and comprehensive approach is needed to drive the collaboration required for transformation.

In addition to successful hiring practices, leaders must cast a net of influence over the entire school district and create a climate where optimism and teamwork thrive. Just as a parent's words and actions shape the climate of the home, the superintendent shapes the atmosphere of the school district. An open, inventive and collaborative culture[2] encourages trust, a necessity for change.

It makes sense, then, that superintendents build an organization of people who are passionately committed to the vision of transformation. For such change-ready people to succeed and thrive, the leader must build an organization, which cultivates and reinforces these values. The organization must be structured so people can thrive and decisions be made by those in closest proximity to the student. Responsibilities and accountabilities are assigned throughout the district to ensure successful transformation. From central administrative offices to individual classrooms, educators must be incented and encouraged to assume responsibilities and make decisions, which benefit the children and fortify transformation objectives. The organizational structure, behavioral practices, and performance criteria must drive alignment of goals and facilitate openness, trust, and collaboration so educators can passionately focus on the heart of transformation—children.

PEOPLE MANAGEMENT DIFFERENCES BETWEEN BUSINESS AND EDUCATION

The CEO and the superintendent ultimately decide how to structure, staff, develop, appraise, and reward performance in the organization. What sets business and education apart is how these vital people management practices are implemented.

STAFFING: RECRUITING THE BEST VS. GETTING THE REST

In most states, large corporations are able to attract top talent with lucrative compensation packages and enticing signing bonuses. As a result, in recent years, most of the best and brightest college graduates have opted to begin their careers in cubicles rather than classrooms. Historically, corporations hired men while top women graduates became teachers. Since the women's rights' movement, corporate careers have opened to women, although teaching positions, especially in elementary schools, continue to be disproportionately filled by women. Corporations now offer women opportunities formerly offered only to men. In part because of corporate hiring and in part as an unintended consequence of the women's movement, the ranks of super teachers in both elementary and secondary schools have been sorely diluted. While there are many outstanding teachers, they now represent the lower third of college graduates.[3]

To combat this trend and to compete with corporations who lure potential math and science teachers, some school districts are offering signing bonuses, alternative certification, and higher initial pay.[4]

Inner city and rural schools have an even more difficult task attracting top graduates since their excellent teachers frequently transfer to suburban schools. To counteract this, programs such as Teach for America[5] seek to attract recruits by exchanging free education and additional pay for a commitment to teach two years in more distressed areas.

Schools not only have difficulty getting the right people, some schools find it even more difficult to release educators when they need to exit the system. In corporations, low-performing employees are let go. While efforts to improve performance are often made, if performance ultimately does not meet job requirements, the employee is released. In education, powerful unions and contract terms often prevent timely staffing changes. Teachers are rarely fired during the course of a normal school year, if at all. About 0.1 percent of tenured teachers get laid off.[6] Poor performers may be moved out of a school, but they are often transferred or even promoted to district headquarters. Given these challenges, it becomes even more critical to have the discipline to only recruit and hire high-quality teachers. While achieving a high-quality staff may take longer, especially in urban districts, high performing schools have figured out ways to ensure high quality teachers form the campus decision-making team and create an environment where weaker teachers either improve or leave.

PERFORMANCE MANAGEMENT: PAYING FOR PERFORMANCE VS. HOPING FOR PERFORMANCE

That school systems must rely on public funds to pay teachers and district personnel creates another significant point of divergence between business and education. Bonuses, gift cards, compensatory time, meals, and sanctioned events are only a few of the ways that companies woo, reward, and retain high-performing employees. The flexibility of common business compensation practices can be illegal practices for school districts. In addition, corporate pay rates have increased significantly when compared to pay rates for school teachers and lower level administrators.

Because of their long history with creative compensation practices, corporations are savvy about compensation management. They know how to link compensation to performance without permanently inflating fixed costs. Corporations typically use well-developed job descriptions and performance metrics to measure each employee's contribution. They pay for individual performance within the context of group performance. "Do *your* job well and *you* will be rewarded," they say. Corporations understand the core competence that drives the business. Engineers who design products for a manufacturing company are valued, well-compensated employees. Teachers who provide the core competence that drives education and learning are often underpaid and undervalued.

The community holds district leaders accountable for student achievement. Schools are expected to educate and students are expected to learn. Each teacher's performance is ultimately evaluated by student achievement and dictates whether the district's most critical performance goals are met. It is challenging to effectively measure performance and accurately evaluate teacher effectiveness, collaboration and support for transformation goals.

More education systems are recognizing that high-quality teachers and school leaders are the cornerstone for education and critical for transformation. Revising restrictive policies, providing bonuses to top teachers based on well-balanced metrics, developing pay for performance systems, and offering career-development opportunities are some of the ways effective school systems are beginning to adapt business practices.

COMPETENCY DEVELOPMENT: ON THE JOB TRAINING VS. IN THE CLASSROOM

While school systems and businesses invest in professional development and training, there tends to be more options and flexibility to deliver and have support on the job in corporate settings than in school systems. Workshops, on-line training, and "On the Job Training" (OJT) are typically offered to corporate employees. Team settings and work groups commonly provide access to peers during the workday. From a technology perspective, corporations expect their employees to be proficient in technology, such as Microsoft tools, spreadsheets, presentations, and company online collaborative tools. In the pilot districts, many school leaders and teachers were lagging in technology proficiency. This is a common problem for many other districts as well.

In education, state regulations can dictate requirements for professional development, which may or may not address the district's weaknesses or individual teachers' developmental needs. Union rules can also influence the type and structure of training. As a result, many school districts do not effectively train faculty and staff in core skills, nor do they necessarily encourage proficiency in non-core skills to improve operational efficiency. An English teacher, for example, may not be computer literate or skillful at integrating technology into the classroom. It is also possible a math teacher with only three hours of math in college may be required to teach additional math courses, in spite of inadequate math knowledge.

When school systems do overcome constraints and invest in teacher, principal, and staff training, ingrained biases and outdated approaches can weaken training effectiveness. Annual contracts can dictate training requirements for every teacher, whether needed or not. At times, in education, training effectiveness seems to be measured by total hours completed rather than the relevance of content or intent to apply back in the classroom. Without guidance from campus leaders, the district's training plan will not satisfactorily address essential teacher needs.

While student teaching provides OJT training, sustaining support is difficult once the graduate is hired into the district. Budget cuts have made it increasingly difficult to commit the time needed to observe and support new teachers. Successful schools districts support new teachers by supplementing traditional professional development with structured collaboration among teachers, conferences, sharing information through school web sites and chat rooms or creating a support system of mentors and coaches.

Additionally, our growing reliance on technology demands that teachers and students be tech-savvy, which is as basic as reading, writing, and arithmetic. With the increasing integration of technology needed in the 21st century classroom, it is going to be even more important to go beyond traditional training and invest in the "in-classroom" support it takes to effectively integrate technology into teaching.

One of the biggest challenges with training in both corporate and school system settings is investing in the application of learning back on the job. In a classroom setting, this is often difficult in that the resources are already stretched. The grants created for the Education Transformation Initiative allocated additional funds for in-classroom follow-up and support. Retired teachers were assigned to co-teach or observe and provide feedback to teachers demonstrating recently acquired skills. Former principals were designated to review school data and follow up with principals on implementing proven practices.

ORGANIZATION STRUCTURE: DECENTRALIZED VS. CENTRALIZED

There is a swinging pendulum in business when it comes to centralization and decentralization of support organizations. Centralized corporate services provided by Human Resources or Information Technology are considered enabling functions and are usually in some type of matrix structure with responsibility to the central organization and the decentralized product or service lines. The product or core business drives the corporation and makes demands of the support organizations. In education, it is all too easy to let centralized functions, such as curriculum, finance, research and evaluation, HR or training, dictate what is happening on the campuses and they are often the furthest removed from the day-to-day student learning. Because it is necessary to coordinate and monitor the patchwork of federal, state, and local regulations imposed on schools, districts have traditionally followed a centralized model. In many districts, high mobility rates[7] necessitate a standardized curriculum. At the same time, there is a disconnect between what is stated by the central organization and what happens behind the school walls and classroom doors.

There must be a balance to ensure the centralized processes are disseminated yet, there is considerable need for flexibility. Each campus is different; what is successful at one campus may not be successful at another. The community, culture, students, and resources available to one campus may not be available to another. There is mounting evidence when principals are adequately trained, given autonomy, and empowered to meet the needs of their staff and community, student performance improves.[8]

The balance between centralized and decentralized has direct implications on whether leaders are constrained or empowered. Add often conflicting influence of regulation and political will and the balance gets even trickier for schools. Where should the lines of power and authority be drawn between the district and individual campuses? How much autonomy should be given to campus leaders? Which decisions should be centralized? The decision influences organizational structure, operating style, and

hiring practices. Impact on student achievement should be the governing factor.

At one end of the spectrum, some schools in Virginia have gone to a centralized model, a cookie cutter approach, which seems to be working. These schools are in a military town, which makes a centralized approach more acceptable. At the other end, in New York City, some 28 entrepreneurial principals had the opportunity to opt into empowerment zones. They were given budget, metrics, and goals, which were more stringent than the rest of the district, and they were given two years to meet them. Results dictated whether they were fired or rewarded. Out of the 28, 26 met the test. Once New York proved their model, they went out to the rest of the principals and said, "You have five years to get yourself to the point you can operate like this. What do you need to get there?"

So, while New York empowered some; others aren't empowered until they prove they can do it. A school district in Texas has "earned empowerment." As principals become more successful, based on a certain score on a series of indices and surveys measuring student growth and school climate, they are allowed to make more decisions.

Whatever the model, it is imperative that the district's hiring practices support their operating style and organizational structure. In the Virginia example, hiring entrepreneurial campus leaders could create a mismatch between the district's style and the educators. Similarly, hiring campus leaders who prefer structure could create another mismatch in the New York model.

 KEY TAKEAWAYS

PEOPLE MANAGEMENT IN EDUCATION AND TRANSFORMATION

▶ The quality of an education system rests on the ability of its teachers and school leaders. Education systems face unique challenges with various regulations from the state and federal government. It is imperative to be able to recruit and hire the best quality teachers and eliminate those who are inefficient.

▶ Effective performance management systems are formed by policies to attract, prepare, support, reward, retain, and advance high-quality teachers.

▶ The central organization has the responsibility to set and disseminate the common framework for curriculum and teaching practices balanced with the input and commitment of those closest to student learning. Collaborating around common goals with central district and school leaders is critical.

▶ The level of authority and autonomy must be commensurate with the capabilities of campus leaders. Weak campus leadership can be offset by a more centralized way of doing things to guarantee consistent results.

▶ The focus for professional development must move from traditional training methods to more "in-classroom" support, especially as the integration of technology into teaching methods increases.

REFLECTIVE QUESTIONS

▶ How do your recruiting practices ensure you are attracting and hiring high-quality teachers, especially in positions or areas that are hard to fill? How does your district partner with universities or other programs aimed at attracting high quality teachers?

▶ How do your performance practices allow you to keep and retain the best people? What practices (e.g. mentoring, innovative contracts, etc.) have your district leaders used or observed in other high performing districts that effectively reduced attrition during the first three years of service?

- ▶ How does your district integrate technology with teaching and learning to promote a positive and innovative environment and reinforce desirable behaviors?

- ▶ How does your district assure professional development addresses your educators' real needs and is ultimately applied in the classroom?

- ▶ How does your district promote collaboration vertically and horizontally within and across schools?

- ▶ How are school goals and expectations tied to performance appraisals, compensation and career development opportunities?

- ▶ What criteria does your district use to determine when decisions should be made centrally or at local campuses?

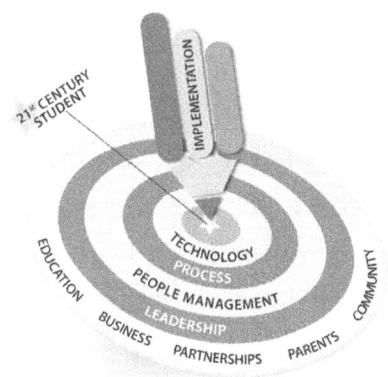

CHAPTER FIVE

ANALYZING HOW THINGS ARE DONE

"To me a leader is someone who holds her- or himself accountable for finding potential in people and processes."
—BRENE BROWN

The Process ring in the Education Transformation Model is heavily intertwined with leadership and strategy, people and organizational structure, technology and the customer. A strategy to improve the customer experience or implement a new technology often requires changes to processes. Likewise, changes to organizational structures can impact responsibilities and shift accountabilities for process execution.

To illustrate the important concept of process, consider a simple example of going out to dinner. To improve a process, it is important to understand the perspective of the customer. The process begins when the customer is greeted upon entering the restaurant and ends when the bill is paid. The overall experience is dependent on how well the process is executed throughout all the steps and people involved. From determining whether or not a reservation was made with the hostess to the timely delivery of a freshly cooked meal from the chef and timely receipt of an accurate bill, the quality of the experience depends on the coordination across the various steps and the people who perform them. If an improvement is identified to reduce wait time by installing a new online reservation system, for example, it is important that the implications of this change be understood and comprehended by all involved in order to ensure the process runs smoothly and that it actually improves the customer experience.

Although processes in business and education are more complicated than this example, the concept is still valid. Transformation requires key processes be analyzed to see if they will work in the new structure and climate. Deciding what core business processes to analyze and improve are critical steps in planning a transformation. Improving those processes is crucial for success.

PROCESS IN TRANSFORMATION

As Michael Hammer and other business process gurus define it, process is a set of interrelated activities aimed at creating a value added output to a customer. Every process starts with input and ends with output and has a series of steps in the middle. The focus in business relates to producing a product, services or a customer. Process in education focuses on improving learning for the student.

Process methodologies share basic principles aimed at deploying a strategy that, with the help of technology, can reduce variability and create substantial improvements. These improvements can potentially help aggressive companies stay on top, transform an organization on the brink of bankruptcy or catapult a low performing school district to new heights. Good processes, in both business and education, make for predictable outcomes and are vital to turning a vision into reality.

PROCESS DIFFERENCES BETWEEN BUSINESS AND EDUCATION

Student learning is a complicated year-over-year process that goes from pre-school to high school, from toddler to teenager. Compare that to the time it takes to complete other "construction" projects. In the late 1800s, the Eiffel tower was built in one year and nine months; the Empire State Building, in exactly 410 days. Today laptops are built in two days to two weeks and cars in one to 24 hours. In contrast, it takes 15 years to educate children from preschool through high school. In business terms, that's a 15-year manufacturing cycle. What business could plan for and survive such a cycle? Yet that is what schools have to do to prepare each student to be college and career ready.

Time isn't the only factor that challenges education and differentiates it from business. Only the best, most suitable raw materials are selected for manufacturing. They are shaped, molded, frozen, heated, and sanitized—according to customer specification and, for the most part, with limited government regulation. Parts are safely stored in a clean room or warehouse, safe from outside contamination. Imperfect items are tossed in a scrap heap. Only flawless, perfect products are offered to the customer.

It is not so easy for education. Children are not perfect and cannot be selected, unless it is a unique school situation and well defined selection criteria. Provided by the community, this source material contains human frailties and strengths. State and federal regulations impact the district's "manufacturing" process. Students cannot stay in a "clean room" and must leave the "manufacturing" facility each day. They go home to life's realities: arguments, sickness, divorce, trauma, abuse, lack of food, and inadequate housing. They return the next day carrying the emotions of the night before mixed in with their textbooks and papers. At the end of each year, individual test scores of every student, not just the gifted ones, measure student learning. Then, the students leave for a two-month break from the rigors of "construction," during which time they lose up two months' worth of what they have learned.[1] After summer break, they come back and the "manufacturing" process starts again, attempting to make up the losses it just suffered. This is a long, daunting 15 years.

The manufacturing analogy emphasizes the sheer complexity of the education process, but it fails to adequately demonstrate the intricate relationship between student and school. Students occupy three overlapping roles. When they are very young and first enter formal schooling, students are the input or source material for the school district. When they graduate from high school, students become the product or output of the district's education processes.[2] As they are progressing through the grades, students are the *target or customer* of the school district, the recipients of the district's products and services. The student in the midst of the process, as the central focus of the schools' efforts, is the object of transformation.

As with the other elements in the model, there are important differences in the business and education approach to process and how these differences affect transformation.

CUSTOMER-CENTRIC: CUSTOMER VS. INTERNAL FOCUS

School districts have long talked about putting the student first and serving the needs of the student, just as businesses cater to the needs of their customers. There is no question that school districts everywhere are dedicated to their students; yet sometimes departmental goals or school boundaries may not support what is needed to ensure every student's success. District leaders may be derailed by unplanned distractions, such as budget crises or compliance issues. Top-down approaches from centralized organizations may divert the laser-like focus, which should be directed at the student, and deflect it on other district priorities. Decisions and directives given to school leaders may make student achievement goals more difficult to attain.

In business, sales teams are responsible for getting additional business, keeping the customer happy and generally advocating for the customer, sometimes going so far as to pressure operations to make changes to satisfy the customer. In public school systems, there is no student advocate or "sales" team responsible for student success and well-being. If schools had such a function, the people responsible would seek feedback to see if decisions and priorities were meeting student needs in the classroom, grade level, and schools across all subjects and aspects of school life. In a student-focused culture, district and campus leaders would partner with students, teachers, principals, and parents and ask: "What do you need? What do the students need? How can we serve you?"

Sometimes non-customer-facing departments in business can lose sight of the customer when internal goals are not aligned. During an early visit to a preK-3 campus, the principal was embarrassed to admit her focus had been on third grade state requirements of reading and math. As part of the reform activities, several of these early primary elementary schools were being converted to preK-5 schools. Given the short-term goals for the third grade and the power of school metrics, she had not focused on getting her students prepared for fourth and fifth grade writing and science. Fortunately as part of the new campus improvement process, the district made preparation for the transition a high-priority. Intense programs were established to re-tool the teachers at all grade levels to increase emphasis in writing and science. In addition, the district was implementing feeder pattern teams with the internal customer, in this case the high school principal, leading collaboration with the campus leaders of the middle schools and elementary schools who would ultimately be responsible for delivering prepared students to the high school. Boundaries must be drawn in any organization, but the key is to ensure mechanisms for collaboration and metrics are in place and aligned to support the "customer."

CROSS-FUNCTIONAL: THE SYSTEM VS. THE SILO

Many large organizations struggle with the complexity of multiple locations, departments, and business units. Manufacturing a product requires the collaboration and coordination of different areas, like design and engineering, quality, manufacturing, marketing, and sales to collectively meet customer requirements.

Large school districts have the same challenge. School buildings and classrooms are physically separate entities that may function almost autonomously. However, even though children are more complex and dynamic than any manufacturer's product, few district-wide processes consider the entire education operation across subjects, grade levels, and schools. Educators still tend to focus on their own subject areas, schools or departments. The public school educational system seems to be designed to reinforce a compartmentalized process of developing math, reading or science curriculum, instead of taking a systemic view across subjects or the entire student learning experience.

To further complicate matters, many of the core educational processes used daily by teachers and principals, such as math and science curriculum or campus improvement processes, are owned by people in the central organization who typically are not directly responsible for delivering them nor is their contribution measured by impact on student learning. It is the teachers and principals who deliver the curriculum, establish the campus improvement plan, and are directly responsible for student learning.

Corporations tend to counter departmental barriers through leadership and joint accountability for goals. Successful businesses tend to assign an influential leader to be responsible and accountable for a cross-functional team charged with fitting the separate pieces together and driving toward process optimization and profits. These owners are measured and rewarded on overall project success and efficiency, not just success and efficiency of one area. If the whole system doesn't work from start to finish or if the customer is not being served, the system is broken.

Successful schools may assign an influential instructional leader to ensure there is alignment across the grade levels for a certain subject. One grade level may run extremely well yet fail to deliver learning that prepares students to be successful in the next grade. Teachers are measured on how well they prepare *their students for the next grade, but rarely is this validated or discrepancies addressed by the teacher at the next level.* This lack of accountability allows the well-oiled, but misaligned third-grade piece mentioned earlier, to be perceived as effective even though it actually contributed to the breakdown of students' successful transition through fourth grade. School and district leaders can collectively establish common, end-to-end expectations and agree on what constitutes success for the whole. Ideally, if students are not prepared for the next level, the environment would be conducive for teachers to be open, collaborate, and determine how to address the situation. Progressive school districts are starting to bridge this gap with a high school feeder pattern approach to promote shared accountability so that students are prepared for the next level.

We worked with two groups within a school district: one was responsible for the district curriculum and the other was responsible for school operations. When we started, the curriculum group would create or change the curriculum and then expect school operations to deploy it. However, school operations didn't know the logic behind the curriculum changes well enough to train their teachers. Operations also believed the curriculum group should deliver the training since they had

made the revisions. The curriculum group thought the school should deliver training since they were going to use the new curriculum. This gap threatened to derail the new curriculum in all schools.

Both group leaders knew the process was broken and both were frustrated with the situation, but neither took the initiative to reach beyond their own organization to solve the problem. We helped both leaders realize that curriculum deployment wasn't going to work well until they acknowledged the problem, aligned expectations, and shared responsibility for successfully implementation and results. We created joint accountability and measured the value teachers received from it.

CONTINUOUS IMPROVEMENT: CONTINUOUS IMPROVEMENT VS STATUS QUO

The drive for continuous improvement, for raising the bar, is inherent to the basic nature of process. Businesses have long been working with this concept.[3] They thrive on getting maximum process efficiency to drive operating costs down and profits up. Businesses are equally concerned with improving the quality of the product itself.[4] Whether driven by the desire to improve or by the natural evolution of events, procedures, and products change. Successes, mistakes, unintended consequences, new technologies, organizational changes, customers, the country's economy—all have the potential to impact existing processes and offer opportunities for improvement. To stay in the game, whether in business or education, processes and products must evolve and improve.

In successful companies, employees at any level may be tasked to figure out more innovative ways of getting work done. Companies focus improvement efforts on areas that are critical to the core business and its customers. They commonly put people from different business units and functions on a team to get end-to-end input and see the big picture. Some companies assign "black belts" trained in lean six-sigma concepts to facilitate teams in removing variability and non-value added steps from their processes. If the team determines critical functions remain unrepresented, the team adds the missing areas until it is complete. In short, the team works together to understand the entire process and come up with precise and clear improvements that reflect their functional interdependency.

> **TO STAY IN THE GAME, WHETHER IN BUSINESS OR EDUCATION, PROCESSES AND PRODUCTS MUST EVOLVE AND IMPROVE.**

There is no doubt educators concentrate on improving their product, which is raising student achievement levels. However, blame tends to be placed on "them" (the students, parents, campus or central function leaders, community or society itself) rather than "us" (teachers, principals, and leaders of centralized functions). School leaders tend to see the successes and failures of the students as the focal point for improvement rather than asking, "What can we do better? What are we missing that is keeping our students from learning?" Educators tend to avoid collaborating on superior ways to produce their product. It is not often educators look for ways to streamline a process or take a process that is working in one subject area and apply it to another subject area. The drive to cut through the bureaucracy and eliminate duplicated efforts is often absent.

In defense of educators, some very real constraints get in the way of streamlining operations. State and federal regulations can make it difficult to change procedures. In addition, much of what goes on in a school district is based on existing practices, or "the way we do things around here," rather than justifiable or legal reasons. An example of this is when a consulting firm came in and wanted to demonstrate how it could add value to the district. The firm's consultants selected a few areas, transportation and legal, and examined the practices. They looked at the employee appeal process that required some 50 steps. On closer examination, they discovered 43 of the steps had been implemented over the years by the legal department, but were not actually required by law. Without these, the number of steps went to seven. That was an eye-opener. The consultants validated a streamlined process not only saves time and money for the legal department, but for parents, students, and the school, as well.

By collectively adapting a more end-to-end view of processes, leaders can be more efficient and develop comprehensive solutions that benefit student learning.

PROCESS IN EDUCATION AND TRANSFORMATION

▶ Process owners are needed to drive end-to-end, district-wide processes that encourage and enable collaboration across department lines, student focus, and collective accountability.

▶ Success is measured and monitored to ensure that student achievement is improving. Well-designed district-wide processes enable predictable and sustainable outcomes from the customer's perspective.

▶ By collectively adapting a more end-to-end view of processes, leaders can eliminate activities that do not add value and develop comprehensive solutions that benefit student learning.

REFLECTIVE QUESTIONS

- ▶ What are your most important processes that facilitate student learning?

- ▶ Are your processes well documented?

- ▶ Who is responsible for managing and improving each process?

- ▶ Are processes aligned and integrated across functions or departments?

- ▶ How well do process measures reinforce desired behaviors among district leaders and employees?

- ▶ Reflect on each key process—who is the customer for each step of the process? How does it contribute to student learning?

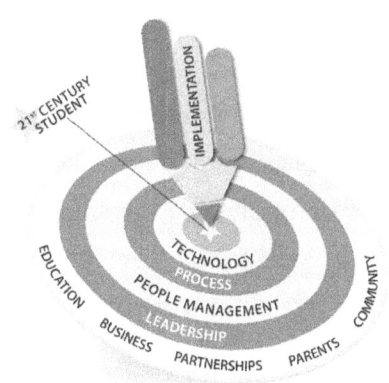

CHAPTER SIX
KEEPING UP WITH THE SPEED OF TECHNOLOGY

"Education is evolving due to the impact of the Internet. We cannot teach our students in the same manner in which we were taught. Change is necessary to engage students, not in the curriculum we are responsible for teaching, but in school. Period."
—APRIL CHAMBERLAIN

The last ring of the Education Transformation Model, Technology, can perhaps be the biggest accelerator of transformation and present the most challenges for leaders, especially in schools. Technology has become an integral and vital part of life. The immense powers of computing are so ingrained in everyday life. The days of manual typewriters, adding machines with rolls of paper memory and inter-office memos filed in in/out boxes have easily faded. Today, Americans connect with their friends, pay bills, and work online. Songs and photos are downloaded wirelessly at home or while sipping coffee at Starbuck®. The latest local or world news, trivia or obscure fun facts can be found online. Smart phones are constant companions. Those who don't have one, lose theirs or leave theirs at home feel alone and isolated. The old mechanical, paper-intensive days are gone. Americans work and play in the digital world as full-fledged technology junkies. Today's children have known no other age than the current one of technology.

For successful transformation to take place in a school district, technology, which is so pervasive and critical in everyday life, must be a key component.

TECHNOLOGY IN TRANSFORMATION

Technology in business and school districts includes technology at the work stations and classrooms, infrastructure that connects and runs the central business systems, collaborative tools for communication, and centralized access to data and information. It also includes social media applications. Social media applications are leaping forward at such a rapid-fire pace that they quickly outdate and outpace written material.

It is enough to say, then, that robust technology infrastructure coupled with centralized data, collaborative tools, and social media applications are critical enablers that can accelerate transformation. However, human factors can turn technology into a double-edged sword. For technology to have an optimal impact, it must be accepted, accessible, and deployed with sufficient training and support. Technology causes competition for attention. With many ways to instantly connect with people, how do we effectively gain and maintain the attention of stakeholders so that our critical messages don't get lost in the noise? How do we keep them focused on transformation priorities when they are constantly bombarded with distractions?

Technology is a critical enabler to 21st century education and to the transformation effort itself. However, it is not an adequate replacement for the face-to-face connection a teacher makes with her students or the personal communication needed to win the hearts and minds of the constituency during transformation.

TECHNOLOGY DIFFERENCES BETWEEN BUSINESS AND EDUCATION

Businesses have long considered technology and the utilization of centralized company data vital to their success and longevity. Technology has transformed business revolutionizing the way work is done. Automation has replaced tedious, manual operations requiring workers to be skilled in running the automation and diagnostics. Without robust infrastructures supporting company-wide systems that produce uniform data, businesses waste precious time and money. In contrast, school districts, in many instances, have lagged behind in the adoption of technology. While financial constraints influence underutilization, they are not the only factor. Underlying attitudes and considerations create differences in the ways business and school districts integrate technology into strategic planning and value it in day-to-day operations.

WILL AND ACCESS: BASIC NEED VS. NICE TO HAVE

Business understands technology can propel it toward the highly sought-after competitive edge. Technology leverages corporate information for its most effective use—to push the company toward profit and peak performance. In addition, technology provides quick, efficient ways for employees to collaborate and communicate. Technology allows customers to shop online and purchase products and services. The estimate is by 2017, 60 percent of U.S. retail sales will involve the internet in some way.[1] For business, technology is not optional; it is vital. They make the investment in infrastructure because it is a requirement to be in business.

Today's children are technology wizards. They carry cell phones, iPods, tablet computers, and portable games. They text and chat online with all their "best friends." In contrast, some school districts lag in the technology adoption curve. Today many elementary or middle schools or even high school classrooms sport little evidence of technology. Although the student-to-computer ratios have increased significantly, many are locked down in a central computer lab or library. If computers are available for students in a classroom, the technology rarely is integrated into the teaching or used for student collaboration. Many teachers still use traditional lectures with transparencies and abundant copies of paper handouts. Electronic boards are being misused as bulletin boards or projection screens. Teachers write key lessons on blackboards and students use pencils to copy them onto paper.

Classrooms and schools are starting to utilize technology increasingly, but to scale the accessibility of technology will require commitment with technology roadmaps that ensure adequate infrastructure and technical support for all students.

It's a mismatch that can threaten the viability of the educational system for the next 100 years. Children are digital; teachers, principals, and district leadership are pen and paper for the most part. It's like outfitting a NASCAR driver with a Soap Box Derby car and expecting him to win the Indy 500. Without the widespread use of technology, schools will not be able to keep the students' interest and student achievement will continue to decline. If a school district isn't trying to determine how to use technology and how to build the infrastructure to take advantage of technological innovations, children will fall even further behind.

For many districts and schools, the capability exists, but there is no systemic commitment to use it. Many teachers are comfortable with paper and pencil and do not have the skills to fully utilize technology or appreciate its potential value. Some very experienced teachers do not use technology and question why they need it. Effectively utilizing technology requires dramatically changing the way teachers teach and students learn.[2] Perhaps some district and school leaders may be hesitant due to the significant investment of time and effort. Some schools are bogged down by the overwhelming tasks confronting them and looking for ways to "just survive." If the public education system is to keep pace with the rest of the world, 21st century schools need to be anchored in technology.

The next challenge for many districts comes down to access to mobile devices and bandwidth. Computers evolved from huge footprints limited to massive data centers to Bill Gates' vision of a personal computer in every household. With the proliferation of more powerful and affordable mobile devices, it is conceivable that every child could have access to a mobile device for appropriate use both inside and outside the classroom. The other limitation for many districts is having a fast and big enough broadband connection. Many schools do not have the bandwidth for large numbers of students to simultaneously utilize the network or the speed to allow for things like downloading videos. Districts and taxpayers must ultimately invest in the infrastructure needed for schools and students learning in the 21st century.

UTILIZATION: NORM VS. EXCEPTION

For many, especially the younger generation, accessing the internet or using a personal computer is second nature. For corporations, being proficient in commonly used software products and online tools is as basic as knowing how to read and write. When new systems or tools are deployed, job-specific training and desk-side support are provided. It is expected that employees use the technology or business applications adopted by the corporation. This is a condition of their employment and necessary in order to do their job.

While schools have certainly advanced beyond the typewriter and the slide rule, many districts have not made technology a foundational element of student learning, a basic tool for community communication, or an integral part of the way work gets done in their school district. While there are tech-savvy teachers who have taken the personal initiative to leverage the power of technology in the classroom, many have not. Too often, students are more tech savvy than their teachers.

There are enough pockets of technology-enhanced teaching to know what this can do for education. With technology, teachers can segment a classroom to work with one group of students while other children are working independently. Lessons can be individualized, self-paced, and self-correcting. Teachers can stop grading math papers when students are given hand-held devices that enable them to submit their answers electronically and get immediate feedback. With technology, students could travel to foreign countries, connect with partner schools, and see outer space, all without leaving the classroom.[3]

When businesses invest in technology, employees are trained and required to master the new systems to gain the benefits they bring. The success of this approach can be seen in the e-retail increase projecting that U.S. consumers will spend $327 billion online in 2016.[4] In contrast, if school districts do adopt new technology, often teacher training is minimal or ineffective and in-classroom support and monitoring is completely missing. The top-down directive requiring teachers to use the new technology gets sidetracked. Instead of innovation or transformation, the status quo is retained and reinforced.[5] The opportunity to use the catalyst for transformation is lost.

The power of technology to radically transform and catapult teaching and student learning into the 21st century is enormous. Think tanks have already begun to see how technology brings the capability to assess students based on competency versus traditional time in seats.[6] Models for effectively teaching with technology must be surfaced and disseminated quickly. Effective dissemination requires investment of time and effort not only into training, but the in-classroom support and coaching needed for teachers to ultimately master and feel confident in teaching. Practice and monitoring the new ways of teaching will be required for the changes to "stick." There is a whole proven methodology around technology deployments engrained in IT practices. This was discussed in the last chapter more around the methodology for implementation.

A misconception I had before becoming a consultant in a public school district was that technology was the primary limitation of technology in schools. However, while providing training and in-classroom support for one technology project, I found over $50K of unopened technology equipment in a school storage room. The valuable equipment was eventually used to expand the program with no additional investment for equipment.

Training teachers on using new technology is often the least appreciated aspect of deploying technology change. If and when training is done, it often consists of the "push-this-button-next" approach. When we asked a group of teachers if they had received training on a new math and science software package for Pre-K students, they all said, "Yes." When we asked if they were using the new software, they answered, "No." Their training did not provide example lessons or demonstrate how age appropriate activities could be incorporated into their existing lessons. When teachers are not confident in operating equipment, they simply find it easier to keep making paper copies than to utilize the equipment in front of their class. When we showed them how to easily draw shapes on a touch board for their class, they became as excited as kids with new techie toys.

One year after moving on to another consulting project, I received a call from a pre-K teacher from the district out of the blue. She had been the recipient of a new electronic white board as part of our technology grant several years ago and along with several of the teachers had unfortunately missed the several hands-on training opportunities availed to them during our time. She was excited to tell me that her new director was very pleased to see the technology at the center and wanted to see the children in action, but she was unable to locate the software and misplaced the directions for using it. Since I never throw anything away, I was able to locate the software and contact information for the online training we had provided so many years ago. Amazing what a little accountability and incentive from leadership can do to drive the use of technology. I was pleased to make the personal visit to deliver the missing software so students would finally be benefiting from the technology—better late than never!

CENTRALIZED INFORMATION: THE BIG PICTURE VS. THE SNAPSHOT

Business invests in technology to build robust performance management systems[7] that run on integrated networks connecting facilities and employees. These systems provide massive amounts of data that is manipulated to produce the information and knowledge to run the business. Business understands the critical two-step combination needed for success: gather data centrally then analyze it to gain company-wide information and knowledge.

Generally speaking, school districts have trouble with this two-step process. Many do not have an integrated technology backbone that encompasses all of their schools and teachers. They tend to have an assortment of stand-alone systems that are accessible to unique groups of educators and that contain an array of disjointed facts. This leads to a lot of data, but little meaningful information. It also leads to a data integrity and data reliability issue.

One data system guru described the school district's data portal as "DRIP—Data Rich and Information Poor." However, after a multi-year investment in data and best practice training plus follow-up with hundreds of campus leaders, district data gurus transformed the data portal. It now gives teachers the ability to look at individual student information and also provides principals with useful information and charts to set realistic goals and identify the strategies to implement, monitor, and achieve the goals throughout the school year. The district appointed a process leader to reinforce the process with district and school leaders to maintain program integrity. The district was able to transform a "check the box" planning activity into a truly data-driven campus improvement process.

KEY TAKEAWAYS

TECHNOLOGY IN EDUCATION AND TRANSFORMATION

▶ Technology improves the "business" of education by providing centralized information systems that produce sound and reliable data so that district leaders can make data-driven financial and operating decisions.

▶ The technology roadmap should enable the district strategy. Ultimately districts must provide access through broadband networks big and fast enough to accommodate video downloads and simultaneous usage by hundreds of classrooms plus arming every student with a mobile device that can be appropriately used inside and outside the classroom.

▶ Districts must support teachers through extensive training and in-classroom coaching where technology is disseminated.

REFLECTIVE QUESTIONS

▶ What is included in your district technology roadmap?

▶ Are your district's systems flexible enough to generate the information necessary to drive informed education decisions?

▶ Do all teachers have adequate training and encouragement to use the technology available? Is equipment utilization expected and reinforced?

▶ What types of processes are in place to support integrating system across the district?

▶ How is technology being effectively utilized in your district? How have teaching practices that effectively integrate technology been disseminated and adopted by teachers across your district or successfully implemented in other districts?

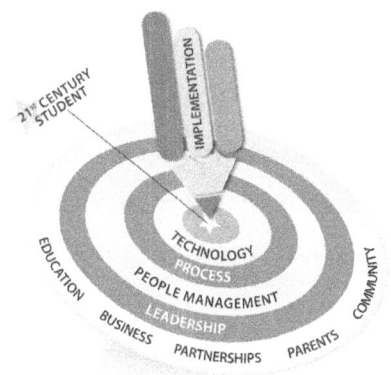

CHAPTER SEVEN
WHERE THE RUBBER MEETS THE ROAD

"Planning without action is futile; action without planning is fatal."
—CORNELIUS FITCHNER

The loftiest transformation vision ultimately comes down to this: getting it done and making it happen. Those simple three-word statements hide a myriad of potholes and speed bumps that can sidetrack even the best transition plans. They can also camouflage cliffs that are steep and deep enough to derail transformation entirely. These barriers can be caused by strong resistance to change, loss of funding or community support, changes in sponsorship or partnership, weakening or change of leadership, unexpected external factors or events, errors in judgment, and miscommunication. Successful transformation maneuvers around the potholes, goes slowly over the speed bumps, avoids the cliffs completely and steadfastly keeps the student as the primary focus.

Despite all the constraints and complexities of the multi-year education process, in spite of regulations, budgets, and changing dynamics, sights must be set on transforming public schools so children can be prepared for the future that awaits them. To miss the mark and allow school systems to remain as they are now, children, and ultimately America, will pay the price.

IMPLEMENTATION IN TRANSFORMATION

Managing the implementation of transformation is like managing the construction of a multi-tier highway intersection without ever shutting down the roadway. The vision for the new intersection must improve traffic flow and relieve congestion. Beyond functionality, the new intersection must suit the surrounding community, protect the safety of the drivers, and generally enhance the quality of their commute. Construction must be completed within a strict budget and must meet government standards. The project must be planned and implemented so as to not impede travel, though it might temporarily slow it, or harm nearby businesses. All aspects of construction must be executed in the right sequence so that bridges, overpasses, access ramps, and highways connect with minimal disruption. Road signs must allow drivers to maneuver through the construction. Information must be readily available so the general community can understand and appreciate the scope, intent, and timing of the project.

As in a construction project, successful school transformation does not just happen. It is a result of a thoughtfully planned and well-executed transition that enables people to achieve desired results. Implementation is the last step in a transformation process. To be successful, transformation needs a strong leader and constituencies who thoroughly understand and agree on the desired end state and are convinced that change is not only needed, but possible. It demands that the interdependencies among people, organizational structures, key processes, and technology are understood and become aligned in a thorough, detailed roadmap for implementation. However, deployment is where the rubber meets the road.

DIFFERENCES IN IMPLEMENTATION BETWEEN BUSINESS AND EDUCATION

Several practices are critical to the journey of transformation in business and education. However, the complexity resulting from the diverse constituencies of a school district impacts how those practices can be applied in education.

SPONSORSHIP: STEADY VS. REVOLVING

Visible and consistent sponsorship is a necessity for any major implementation whether in business or education. Having credible leaders speak clearly and consistently about why change is necessary and what it means to the organization makes the difference between getting a clean start and stumbling out of the blocks.

Business leadership tends to remain relatively steady and emphasize succession planning to ensure smooth leadership transition. In contrast, the churn created by leadership turnover is often a challenge in large urban education systems.[1] Sponsorship must be secured and reinforced across the organization; it must endure over time for true transformation to be safeguarded. In addition, the transition must be clearly understood and translated to all stakeholders, groups who will be impacted and even those who believe they will be impacted by the change. Focus groups and other forums can be hosted to check for stakeholder understanding and buy-in. Clearly articulated direction helps ensure alignment of leaders internally and externally; it can also generate trust that can be leveraged should leadership changes occur. Every time there is a change in leadership, the momentum of the transformation is at risk. Everyone watches to see whether the transformation goals are among the priorities of the new leader. Building a coalition with a broad base of influential leaders, both internally and externally, is one way to weather the storms that often come with leader changes.

RESOURCES: NECESSITY VS. LUXURY

In business it is common for an executive leadership team to establish a project team with a mix of expertise needed to implement a transition. Since this expertise may not be part of the core competency of the business, external resources, which can supply objectivity and additional capacity, are brought into the project team. Depending on the size of the transformation, the core team typically consists of an influential business leader, plus a few key roles dedicated to executing the project.

The project manager is responsible for developing a detailed resource plan and timeline ensuring the plan is executed on time and within the budget allocated by the executive leadership team.

A change management expert is another critical role brought in to work closely with the business leader and project team to analyze the impact on people and ensure that the project team addresses valid reasons for resistance during implementation. Often this includes devising a plan for engaging, communicating, training, and ensuring the people in the organization are prepared and accepting of the new way of working.

Often technology is a key enabler for transformation and a technical lead is assigned to the project team. The technical lead ensures that the new technology does what it is intended to do and that it is integrated into the operational infrastructure.

While these roles are common for large-scale transformations in business, the understanding of the importance of these roles during major transitions in education is not well recognized. Perhaps budget constraints come into play. These roles are not typically found within the school systems and taking counsel from non-educators may be seen as a barrier. However, if there is a commitment to change, dedicated resources for implementation are needed to guide and reinforce transformation. Few people in the district have the time, authority or skills to identify all the disjointed pieces of the puzzle across the district and manage the white space to pull them together without biasing the outcome. As in the example of the intersection construction, coordination and collaboration are necessary across the district to keep the community informed and avoid unnecessary disruptions.

ENGAGEMENT: STRUCTURE VS. "IT HAPPENS"

Committed leadership and a project team alone will not create transformation. If raising just one child takes a "village," imagine how many people it will take to transform and sustain transformation in a school district with thousands of children. Understanding how transformation impacts all the constituents and stakeholders is the first critical requirement for success. The next, and the more difficult, is ensuring all constituents and stakeholders are appropriately engaged throughout the entire implementation.

While transformation is like a massive construction project, it is inherently more complicated because transformation leaders are not working with concrete and steel that stay in place once they have been formed or molded. The building blocks of transformation are ever moving and morphing: students, parents, school boards, businesses, community leaders, the news media, and unions. Transformation leaders must be willing to hear concerns and have the ability to activate people of influence across all stakeholder groups to collectively agree to common, well defined goals and an implementation plan to achieve them.

Communication and community engagement are key ingredients to keep all constituents connected, informed, and involved in the transformation. Communication is not a casual after-thought or by-product, but a planned activity that supports and reports on each aspect of transformation. Without engagement and communication tailored to each constituent group, transformation won't be readily understood or accepted. A flashy, interactive, high-tech web site filled with the most critical transformation information is useless to parents who don't have access to the internet. Communication between the district and all constituents needs to flow bi-directionally and constantly so concerns are addressed in a timely manner and public opinion remains solidly behind the effort.

I worked with a school district that had a diverse student population and wanted to hold a series of parent communication sessions. We knew we needed to respect the cultures represented in the district and create communication approaches for the parents rooted in their own cultural practices. Our solution to the potential problems associated with cultural variation was to contract with a community activist from the African-American community and another from the Latino community. In assembling the communication sessions, we provided each of the community activists with a small budget and the express goal of getting as

many parents as possible to attend the meeting. The African-American activist frequented the local churches and the barber and beauty shops because that is where urban African-American parents were. The Latino activist went to the Catholic Church, several large Hispanic organizations and a few quinceañeras[2] to contact the parents. Because the approach to recruitment for each of the meetings was fundamentally different, the parent sessions were very well attended and highly successful.

ROADMAP: FRUITION VS. FORGOTTEN

Most leaders in education and in business can recognize the need to change and can devise a sensible plan. Too often, though, there is a breakdown at the intersection of creation and implementation where the challenge shifts from "what" to "how." Once the roadmap is created and implementation begins, it has to be executed, monitored, and adjusted to overcome unforeseen issues as they arise. Roadblocks emerge and the resolve to navigate around them is tested. Resources assigned to manage the roadmap must not only be skilled enough to execute the plan, but also resilient enough to traverse the potholes and landmines along the way. The executive leadership must be integral to expediting decisions, removing roadblocks and ensuring the long-term commitment required for the transformation to be successful.

It seems the hurdles can become higher and the potholes, deeper for school systems than for business. Business runs on a full fiscal year broken into quarters mainly for the purpose of financial reporting. There is no real break or distinction in activities between quarters. On the other hand, most school districts still run on a nine-month school year with a distinct beginning, middle, and end interrupted with a planned summer break. Between school years, staffing and students change. Therefore, key implementation activities must be performed in this shorter, nine-month time frame. In addition, because of the summer break, more monitoring and adjusting is required to ensure that all new stakeholders are on board and that the project stays on track over the years.

A transformation roadmap overseen by a committed executive group of decision-makers and executed by a dedicated project management team is critical to each stage of implementation being completed on time, within budget, and, most importantly, achieving results that "stick."

It ultimately boils down to execution—getting it done—in every district, campus, classroom, and with every student. Successful implementation requires a methodical approach, dedicated resources, and a long-term commitment—this is the "science" and expertise business consultants and change management professionals bring.

Only when the superintendent takes hold of the arrow, aims, and shoots can the bullseye be hit. The passion and desire to win—to see students compete with the best in the world and be prepared for the 21st century—must start with the leader. There is nothing more important to the future of education than strong leadership that "walks the talk" and are role models for transformation.

IMPLEMENTATION IN TRANSFORMATION

▶ Transformation begins with visible, active leadership and a clear direction. It must be understood across leadership and key stakeholders.

▶ Transformation roles must be clearly defined and appropriately resourced with influential education leaders and implementation experts and a commitment for the long haul.

▶ The project team must engage all stakeholder groups to understand the valid reasons for resistance and ensure they are addressed to proactively manage the transition.

▶ Children are the future. Doing the right things at the right times are crucial. The time is now to make the commitment for transformation in education.

REFLECTIVE QUESTIONS

- How have you defined success for your transformation effort?
- What resources have been dedicated to the implementation of your transformation effort?
- List the different groups who will be impacted by decisions in your school district? What are their expectations and concerns?
- Has a communication plan been developed to ensure all key stakeholders understand and accept the transformation? What are the key concerns and messages for each stakeholder group?
- What type of ongoing reviews and evaluations are in place to ensure the change "sticks" and is not short lived?
- How has the transformation team been empowered to make decisions and get results?

CHAT ROOM

In many gyms, there are signs such as the one that reads, "Never let weakness convince you that you lack strength." Those words may have initially come from a sage philosopher commenting on the strength of the human spirit or a bulked-up weight lifter who had a bad day at the gym. They also accurately reflect our attitude toward the possibility of transformation in education. Weakness, and even failure, in the modern education system does not mean a lack of strength. Many educators are dedicated and committed to serving the student. They believe change can and will happen. Many community and business leaders passionately support the efforts of public schools. They can and will influence and spur transformation. Many parents are willing to work with their neighborhood schools to improve the lives of their children. They believe their schools will get better.

We acknowledge the weaknesses, but believe in the strength we collectively possess. We must have the courage to pull back the bow, aim the arrow, and hit the bullseye for education transformation. For the success of our children, we must take action.

CONCLUSION

WHAT WE BELIEVE

*"Let us not be content to wait and see what will happen,
but give us the determination to make the right things happen."*
—PETER MARSHALL

There is dire need for education reform and transformation. As leaders in education and business, we must either bridge the gap or accept responsibility for our negligence. America's school systems and this country's future in the global community are at great risk if we do not dramatically change the way we educate our children.

Transforming education is a daunting, complex task which demands vision, leadership, commitment, persistence and patience. It is an effort that takes more than hope, and in many instances, takes more than a village.

There are no magic wands or silver bullets. Even so, transformation can be achieved if we will work together and utilize proven change management practices to mitigate risks and withstand the chaotic journey of transformational change.

Competitive American businesses have been transforming for years with great success. From culture changes to product changes, technology changes and changes in competition, markets, and environments, American business has adapted and thrived using recognized change management processes. As our experience demonstrates, when these practices are adapted properly, these processes and practices are just as relevant in education.

Margaret Mead said, "Never doubt that a small group of thoughtful committed citizens can change the world; indeed, it's the only thing that ever has." If not here, where? If not now, when? If not us, who?

Take on the challenge of transforming your district ... whether you are a reform advocate in the community, a consultant working on implementing a new program in a school, or a district leader courageously preparing your students for the 21st century. Join with other like-minded people in learning how to effectively manage transformational change. Engage and make a difference for your school. The children need you.

In closing, we hope that something in this book has piqued your interest or even motivated you to take on the challenge of transforming your district. If you are on a journey or thinking about taking on change and need advice or assistance with your plan or vision, contact us. Our bios and contact information are provided at the back of this book. In the end, it is our hope that true change and transformation can be realized for the children, who are America's future.

ENDNOTES

CHAPTER ONE

1. Brownstein, Ronald. "National Journal." NationalJournal.com. National Journal, 16 Apr. 2012. Web. 20 Dec. 2013.

2. Gaskill, Adi. "Is Facebook's Member Growth Slowing?" SDLSM2.com, Social Media Analysis, Web. 11 June 2012 at 1:24 pm.

3. Yardley, Joseph Kahn And Jim. "As China Roars, Pollution Reaches Deadly Extremes." The New York Times. The New York Times, 26 Aug. 2007. Web. 18 Dec. 2013.

4. Henry Ford and Thomas Edison involved in significant innovation at the turn of last century.

5. In the short history of the PC, several names have been associated with its invention. Though not the original inventors, Steven Jobs and Stephen Wozniak, both of California popularized the computer with their invention of the Apple II in 1977.

6. Theodore Maiman is credited with making the first laser operate on May 16, 1960, at the Hughes Research Laboratory in California.

7. Consistently low performing schools can be closed by the state or school district, but generally speaking, schools cannot refuse to educate students.

8. College and Career Ready (CCR) is the current standard of student achievement in public education.

9. The Council of the Great City Schools is a coalition of 66 of the nation's largest urban public school. Founded in 1956 and incorporated in 1961, the Council is located in Washington, D.C., where it works to promote urban education through legislation, research, media relations, instruction, management, technology, and other special projects designed to improve the quality of urban education.

10. Casserly, Michael. Beating the Odds. Council of the Great City Schools, Mar. 2003.

11. "Unite to Make a Difference Forum 2011." USA Today and Council of the Great City Schools,18 Mar. 2011.

12. The PISA exam is one of a handful of tests that compare educational levels across nations, and it is considered the most comprehensive. Associated Press. "In Ranking, U.S. Students Trail Global Leaders." Latest World & National News & Headlines. USA Today, n.d. Web. 20 Dec. 2013.

13. Hanusek, Erik A., Paul E. Peterson and Ludger Woessman. "Is the U.S. Catching Up?" RSS. Education Next, 7 July 2012. Web. 20 Dec. 2013. Hanusek, Erik A., Paul E. Peterson and Ludger Woessman. International and U.S. State Trends in Student Performance, pp. 4-5. Harvard's Program on Education Policy and Governance and Education Next. Harvard Kennedy School.

14. Duncan, Arne. Interviewed by Gwen Ifill, Recorded Interview. Education Town Hall. Newseum, Washington, D.C. December 7, 2010.

15. Casserly, Michael. Beating the Odds. Council of the Great City Schools, Mar. 2003.

CHAPTER TWO

1. Hamel, Gary; Prahalid, C.K. "The Core Competence of the Corporation." Harvard Business Review, (May-June 1990). Stroupa, Alex. "10 Reasons Why DCA is a Bad Idea – Part Two." Harvard Business Review, (10 August 2000).

2. "Results from PISA 2012—United States Key Findings." OECD: Better Policies for Better Lives. OECD, 13 Dec. 2013. Web. 20 Dec. 2013. "Among 34 OECD countries, the United States performed below average in mathematics in 2012 and is ranked 26th. Performance in reading and science are both close to the OECD average. The United States ranks 17 in reading and 21 in science. There has been no significant change in these performances over time.

3. Tom Luce, co-founder of NCEA and sponsor of the Just For The Kids School Improvement Model, a framework for schools to increase levels of college and career readiness. The framework utilizes research-based, data-driven solutions based on best practices.

4. "Program Overview." Texas Higher Education Assessment. N.p., n.d. Web 20 Dec. 2013. Since 1989, the Texas Higher Education Assessment® (THEA®) has provided Texas students and institutions of higher education with a flexible, fair, and accurate testing and score-reporting system. Its purpose is to assess the reading, mathematics, and writing skills that entering freshman-level students should have if they are to perform effectively in undergraduate certificate or degree programs in Texas public colleges or universities.

5. "ACT, Ready for College or Ready for Work: Same or Different?" 2006. N.p.: n.p., n.d. N. pag. Print.

6. The Broad Prize is awarded each year to honor urban school districts that demonstrate the greatest overall performance and improvement in student achievement while reducing achievement gaps among low-income and minority students.

CHAPTER THREE

1. We refer to the CEO and superintendent as singular leadership entities throughout this section for the sake of clarity and simplicity.

2. A sampling of some of the recommended authors included Warren Bennis, Peter F. Drucker, Max De Pree, Jim Collins, John William Gardner, Peter M. Senge, James M. Kouzes, Barry Z. Posner, Kenneth H. Blanchard, John P. Kotter and Spencer Johnson.

3. Porter, M.E. "How Competitive Forces Shape Strategy," Harvard Business Review, (March/April 1979).

4. The bell shaped curve is a common description of the graph (that is in the shape of a bell) representing a normal distribution in probability theory. In a standard normal distribution (or bell curve), most of the variables will group around or center on the mean or the middle, at the peak of the bell curve. Those variables outside of the middle will taper off at either end, leaving two smaller, narrower tails.

5. Only one out of 11 "Good-to-Great" companies hired executives from outside. Collins, James C. "Appendix 2A." Good to Great: Why Some Companies Make the Leap—and Others Don't. New York, NY: HarperBusiness, 2001. N. pag. Print.

6. "The Conference Board." Press Releases. N.p., 12 Apr. 2012. Web. 20 Dec. 2013.

7. Payzant, Tom. "Students Need Stable District Leadership." District Administration Magazine. N.p., Mar. 2012. Web. 20 Dec. 2013.

8. "Students Need Stable District Leadership." District Administration Magazine. N.p., n.d. Web. 24 Feb. 2014.

CHAPTER FOUR

1. Collins, Jim. *Good to Great*. Harper Collins Publishers, NY. 2001. Good to Great identifies five characteristics found in great companies. In the section on leadership, when Collins discusses the importance of assembling the right team, he contends that a leader needs "to get the right people on the bus."

2. Sometimes the use of the word culture causes discomfort because it is a "soft" word that can have multiple meanings. Here culture means the climate or operating style of a school district or community. Operating style is discussed at length later in the chapter.

3. Augusta, Bryon, Paul Kihn, and Matt Miller. "Insights & Publications." Attracting and Retaining Top Talent in US Teaching. p. 12., Sept. 2010. Web. 2 Jan. 2011.

4. Dempsey, Bobbi. "Best States for Teachers." Investopedia. N.p. 14 May 2010. Web. 20 Dec. 2013.

5. Teach For America provides well-trained teachers to underserved communities, with the goal of helping break the cycle of educational inequity. Teachers in the program commit to teaching for two years in one of 39 urban and rural regions across the country, going beyond traditional expectations to help their students to achieve at high levels. Founded in 1990, there are now more than 8,200 teachers, 20,000 alumni, 500,000 students impacted annually and over three million students reached.

6. McGuinn, Patrick. "Ringing the Bell for K-12 Teacher Tenure Reform." Drew University and Institute for Advanced Study. February 2010. The March 15, 2010, edition of Newsweek contained an article titled, "Why We Must Fire Bad Teachers." The article reported the percentage of tentured teachers who were dismissed for poor performance. The 0.1 percent we used is the highest rate of the five U.S. cities cited. The actual numbers Newsweek cited included: New York City, 2008, three out of 30,000; Chicago, 2005-2008, 0.1 percent; Toledo, .01 percent; Akron and Denver, 0 percent. The article also contended "about 99 percent of all teachers in the United States are rated 'satisfactory' by their school systems." "Table 8. Average Number of Public School Teachers and Average Number of Public School Teachers Who Were Dismissed in the Previous Year or Did Not Have Their Contracts Renewed Based on Poor Performance, by Tenure Status of Teachers and State: 2007-2008." Table 8. Average Number of Public School Teachers and Average Number of Public School Teachers Who Were Dismissed in the Previous Year or Did Not Have Their Contracts Renewed Based on Poor Performance, by Tenure Status of Teachers and State: 2007-2008. U.S. Department of

Education, 2007-2008. Web. 20 Dec. 2013. Data from the U.S Department of Education's 2007-2008 Schools and Staffing Survey reveal that on average, school districts dismiss or decline to renew, only 1.4 percent of tenured teachers each year.

7. In urban school districts mobility rates of 40 percent are common, which says that in a school district of 200,000 children, some 80,000 relocate within the school district each year. One cause for high mobility rates is that low-income parents tend to follow apartment rent specials. If Johnny started learning how to add primary numbers on Tuesday, and his parents move to a new apartment, Johnny needs to continue learning how to add primary numbers in his new school on Wednesday.

8. William G. Ouchi addresses school decentralization in his two books. In Making Schools Work, he found that when principals were given autonomy over their schools, the performance of those schools improved measurably. In The Secret of TSL, he explains what autonomous principals do to improve their schools and demonstrates that there is a direct correlation between how much control a principal has over his or her budget and how much that school's student performance rises.

CHAPTER FIVE

1. According to the John Hopkins University Center for Summer Learning, all students experience learning losses when they do not engage in educational activities during the summer. On average, students lose approximately 2.6 months of grade level equivalency in mathematical computation skills during the summer months. Low-income students experience greater summer learning losses than their higher income peers.

2. The analogy could continue further. The output of high school, the graduates, becomes the input for colleges. Then, college graduates become the input for the job market.

3. We have listed some of the books we like on process change and management: Business Process Change, Second Edition: A Guide for Business Managers and BPM and Six Sigma Professionals, (the MK/OMG Press) by Paul Harmon; Business Process Management, Second Edition: Practical Guidelines to Successful Implementations by John Jeston; Process Mapping, Process Improvement and Process Management by Dan Madison.

4. Stephen Covey, in his 1990 book, Seven Habits of Highly Effective People, refers to this as production capability vs. production.

CHAPTER SIX

1. "60% of U.S. Retail Sales Will Involve the Web by 2017." E-Commerce Sales. N.p., n.d. Web. 26 Mar. 2014.

2. We recognize that many school districts do passionately look for leading-edge innovations to stimulate learning. We are referencing attitudes that exist in schools and classrooms we have worked with and that are prevalent enough to mention.

3. Kahn Academy provides free online lessons and resources for students and teachers.

4. Rueter, Thad. "E-retail Spending to Increase 625 by 2016." Industry Statistics. Internet Retailer, 27 Feb. 2012. Web. 20 Dec. 2013. Forrester analyst Sucharita Mulpuru says it derives its estimates by analyzing trends in the monthly retail sales figures released by the U.S. Census Department.

5. Technology approaches and practices can be different for private and public magnet schools, which generally attract a more elite student population, have more resources, and a greater degree of parental and community involvement than the other schools.

6. Horn, Michael; Shelton, Jim; Silva, Valerie; Witt, Alex; Clinton, Chelsea. "Digital Divide, Equity and Access." Education Nation. MSNBC. MIT Town Hall, Boston, MA. 13 Sept. 2012. Town Hall Meeting.

7. These are enterprise-wide systems that track metrics and performance. They are used in areas as performance management, human resources and product information.

CHAPTER SEVEN

1. "The Conference Board." Press Releases. N.p., 12 Apr. 2012. Web. 20 Dec. 2013. Article references 8 year average for CEO's of Corporation. Payzant, Tom. "Students Need Stable District Leadership." District Administration Magazine. N.p., Mar. 2012. Web. 20 Dec. 2013. Article references 3.6 average year term for CGSC superintendents.

2. A quinceañera—"quince" representing the number 15 in Spanish—is a coming-of-age ritual for many Hispanic girls. Similar to the more family American version of the sweet 16 party, family and friends gather to celebrate a girl's passage to adulthood. Festivities can include a church service, dinner, dancing, and other local traditions. The young girl making the transition generally dons a formal gown and is accompanied by several young men invited to escort her. Quinceañera parties serve as important community events within many Hispanic communities, where members of a neighborhood, town, or city come together to honor the transformation of a girl into a woman.

GOOD PROCESSES, IN BOTH BUSINESS AND EDUCATION, MAKE FOR PREDICTABLE OUTCOMES AND ARE VITAL TO TURNING A VISION INTO REALITY.

MARCIA PAGE

Marcia Page, President and CEO of Education is Freedom, has extensive experience in urban education, educational technology, and government processes. She served as President and CEO of the Foundation for Community Empowerment in Dallas, TX, as a loaned executive from Texas Instruments, where she held an officer position for sixteen years.

Page is known for her ability to quickly grasp the big picture, work collaboratively, and develop processes that get results. She is high energy and has the intellectual horsepower to grasp new concepts and business models and be decisive in a fast-paced, multifaceted organization.

In addition to her professional qualifications, Page is passionate about creating and fostering real change in the urban educational system. As a testament to her dedication to help urban schools, despite her other accomplishments (including the Malcolm Baldridge Award), she is most proud of the Scholarship Program endowed by Texas Instruments for African American Females demonstrating excellence in Mathematics, Engineering and Technology.

She holds a B.S. in Management and Organizational Behavior with emphasis in Accounting and Computer Science from the University of Nebraska at Omaha. She has earned management certifications in Governmental Policies and Practices from Harvard University and Business Strategy from the University of Indiana.

marcia.page@att.net | Email
972/979-5359 | Phone

JOAN NICHOLS

Joan Nichols, Managing Partner of JNichols & Associates and seasoned change agent, exudes a unique blend of practical business experience coupled with a passion and energy for leading people though large-scale transformation efforts. Her ability to quickly develop relationships, assess an organization and connect to the business strategy has allowed her client base to span across industries from semiconductor, manufacturing, and insurance to education and non-profit.

Prior to her consulting career, Nichols spent over seventeen years with Texas Instruments in organizational change management. She led transformation efforts across the corporation including several company mergers, ERP system implementations, and customer service process redesigns leading to significant business results including revenue growth, reduced costs, improved customer perceptions and employee satisfaction.

She holds a Masters in Organization Development and Change Management from University of Texas-Dallas, a B.S. in Industrial Engineering from University of Missouri, and certifications in Myers Briggs Type Indicators, Accelerating Change, and PDI Profilor.

j.nichols4@yahoo.com | Email

PATTI WATERBURY

Patti Waterbury, Founder of Creative Growth Strategies, is a transformation speaker and business coach accelerating growth and outcomes through biblical principles, proven business methods, and behavioral practices that transform leaders and systematically improve business results. In addition to best sellers, *Unbreakable Spirit* (co-authored with Lisa Nichols) and *The Next Big Thing—Top Trends from Today's Leading Experts to Help You Dominate the New Economy*, she is also featured as one of 40 amazing women of courage in *Fearless Women: Fearless Wisdom*.

Building on a Masters in Organizational Development and Change Management, she is perpetually learning from thought leaders of the day. With more than twenty years as an organizational troubleshooter and executive coach to Fortune 500 business leaders, entrepreneurs, and directors of nonprofit organizations, her diverse academic background and experience give her a unique ability to discern core problems, clarify choices, and guide decisions.

www.pattiwaterbury.com

**WE MUST HAVE THE COURAGE TO
PULL BACK THE BOW,
AIM THE ARROW,
AND HIT THE BULLSEYE FOR
EDUCATION TRANSFORMATION.**

www.ingramcontent.com/pod-product-compliance
Lightning Source LLC
LaVergne TN
LVHW021356080426
835508LV00020B/2296